Roots of My Identity

 Beyond The Book Media, LLC Alpharetta. GA www.beyondthebookmedia.com **ISBN: 978-1-953788-33-7 (Printed)**

Roots of My Identity

Michele Altman

"Trust in the Lord with all your heart and lean not on your own understanding; in all your ways submit to Him, and He will make your path straight"

(Proverbs 3:5-6, NIV).

I would like to give all praise, honor, and glory to my Lord and Savior, Jesus Christ. If it were not for Your love, grace, and mercy I would not be here today. Thank You for leaving the ninety-nine to come to rescue the one (me).

TABLE OF CONTENTS

Thank you to my children, Marcellus, Ayanna, and Tiera. Thanks for begin my biggest cheerleaders, and never giving up on me. Let God forever be your anchor. I love you!

A special thank you to Nancy Zimmermann - my sister in Christ, friend, and my person. Thanks for encouraging me to tell my story.

Jake Cheesbrough, and Linda Oberbrunner for your honest input.

Thank you to Chanel Martin, and the entire Beyond the Book Media Team. So glad I watched that Facebook live!

"Sometimes it's not the times you decide to fight, but the times you decide to surrender, that make all the difference." - Courtney Praski

Book Endorsements

I never tire of hearing Michele's story. It is a word of hope for the brokenness in and around you. It will encourage you to speak life and truth to those you love. It will remind you of who God says you are. You will see how God wastes nothing in the lives of His children and be inspired to do something great for Him.

-Nancy Zimmermann, President of Cornerstone of Grace (and Michele's sister in heart)

Roots of My Identity is a memoir that manages to take you inside the mind of its author, Michele Altman. Altman breaks up the book into different sections of her life and the trials and tribulations that arose from various events. Altman manages time and time again to subvert expectations by turning to different aspects of her life without divulging anything before the specific event happens. Because Altman chose to tell the story this way, the heartbreaking, shocking, tearful, uplifting, and empowering moments are all felt with a blunt ferocity. This approach truly helps the reader feel as Altman felt in those moments and experience them as she lived them.

The memoir's nonfiction narrative is overlaid with a spiritual nature throughout but what is so impressive is that her story does not "rely" on this to carry it. Altman's story is equally as compelling for those who are not spiritual in nature.

Altman's story of life and the obstacles she overcomes make the memoir so difficult to put down and have you wish–more than you could have imagined while picking up this book–to have her surrender the madness by the end of it.–Jake Cheesbrough

Real, revealing, and relevant, all describe the redemptive journey of Michele Altman in Roots of My Identity. Her forthright account details the joy and heartache she experienced as a young child. This riveting narrative also includes the deep pain of loss and the severe consequences of poor choices. Full restoration through Christ becomes evident after Michele receives and understands the grace, mercy, and blessings she was told about as a child. This is a rewarding read that will touch your heart and soul.

Linda Oberbrunner, Author Mercy Extended, Social Worker

INTRODUCTION

"Welcome to Burger King. How may I help you?"
"May I get a double Whopper, with cheese, off the broiler, with bacon, and extra mayo, a large fry, and a chocolate shake?"

Personally, I love a good burger. Burger King was always my first choice when I wanted one. I enjoyed going to Burger King because one, it was delicious, and two, you could order a burger to your specific liking. Plus, it supported my mantra of life -- "Have it your way." Who doesn't want it their way? I know I did. I did what I wanted when I wanted, and how I wanted. Having it my way was how I chose to do life. I quickly found out doing things my way would lead me down the wrong path. There was a battle going on for my identity. I battled with who people said I was. I battled with who I believed I was. I fought these battles all while struggling to overcome drug addiction. With all these competing perspectives, which one would I believe?

My belief system was structured on what I was told I could and could not do. As a child, I was fed words of life and words of death. I felt the words of death smothered the words of life. The words spoken over me would define the person I would become.

The words spoken over me would mold the choices I would make. The words spoken over me would encourage my perception of how I viewed myself. The words planted in my childhood shaped the roots of my identity.

What was spoken over and over, I began to believe. When I began to believe what was said, I began to walk in that belief. The negative words became my negative thoughts. Thoughts are powerful. Those negative words became my thoughts and eventually became my words. "The words you say will either acquit you or condemn you" (New Living Translation, Matthew 12:37). Those negative thoughts then produced negative life choices, and then my negative life choices began to spiral out of control. I chose to live life the way I wanted. I began to travel down a road of madness, addiction, and despair. This world of madness became a battlefield for my identity, my purpose, and my life.

The enemy had me surrounded. The battlefield was a kill zone and was set up to destroy and conquer me. Death and destruction were all around. I never knew what was waiting for me around the next corner. I was wounded and there was bloodshed everywhere. I was not prepared to fight this battle. I had no defense. I didn't know if I should continue to fight or raise the white flag of surrender.

I would never have imagined myself on drugs, a prostitute, and living in a world of madness, but that was the battlefield I found myself on.

CHAPTER 1

MY UP BRINGING

My childhood was good. I had two loving and supportive parents. My parents seemed to be happy. My mom was beautiful. She nurtured me in many ways. She encouraged, spent quality time, and sang songs to me. My mom was also a talented seamstress. I remember having the most stunningly unique dresses. I always looked forward to picture day because I knew my dress would look like no one else's.

The dress I remember the most was yellow with faint shades of blue flower patterns with a headband to match. It was my princess dress. I loved to dance and spin around in it. At the age of seven, my mom bought me my own little sewing machine, and I would sew little outfits, with her help, for my baby dolls. I also liked being in the kitchen while she cooked. The smells she would have coming from that kitchen were amazing! Freshly baked bread, homemade German chocolate cake, pot roast with potatoes and carrots, greens, or my favorite baked macaroni and cheese. Meals were always good, made from scratch, and with love at our house. However, the thing I remember most about my mom is how loving and kindhearted she was.

She continuously showed me that she loved me. She showed affection both through words and gestures. She would rub my face, stroke my back, and tell me multiple times a day how special I was and how much she loved me. I could even see the love in her eyes. Her eyes filled with joy whenever she looked at me. Even when she scolded me, I knew she loved me.

My mom would tell me to love and respect people for who they were. She would say we were all created by God. "Do not treat people based on how they look or what they may be going through. Always try to treat people how you want to be treated, even when it's hard." She was big on family. She made sure the entire family sat down weekly and ate a meal together.

I was raised in a Christian home, at least on my mom's side. My mother's actions matched what a follower of Jesus should be. We went to church; she sang in the choir, and she helped people out when they needed help. Plus, she spent time with God. She read her Bible, I heard her pray, talk to Him throughout the day, and she got her praise and worship on. My mom modeled daily how to let God into every area of life. She was the most loving person I knew. She also instilled the importance of keeping God in everything we did. She would often tell me that I was the apple of God's eye. I asked her what "being the apple of God's eye" meant. She said, "You are special to God. He loves you and will always protect you." I knew without question I was loved. She earnestly loved God, her family, and others.

My dad loved me as well, but he showed it differently. My dad was always the breadwinner. He was also very stern. He was a man of order and wanted things to reflect as such. He worked hard and provided for his family extremely well. Instinctively, he was not a very affectionate man. But with me, he had no choice but to love on me because I would climb onto his lap and lay in his arms for hours. We didn't have to be doing anything for me to feel content. I only wanted to be around him.

I vividly remember my mom telling me one Saturday morning to put on a shirt and some shorts because we were going to the amusement park with my aunt and her children. Most kids would be ecstatic about spending the day riding Ferris wheels, eating cotton candy, and having a day of fun. However, my response was, "Is my daddy coming with us?" The answer was no. I considered it a day of fun when I was in the presence of my daddy. I quickly asked him if I could stay home with him. Thankfully, he said yes.

My dad loved drinking coffee. That day was the first of many days he would give me coffee in a dixie cup. I was his baby girl, and I had his heart. I could pretty much ask for whatever I wanted and get it. I was spoiled. I seemed to cling more to him than my mom. I never understood why. I honestly enjoyed being in his company; that was good enough. I felt safe with him.

I do not remember him traveling to church with us very often. Sometimes on holidays, he would join us. I do not remember seeing him have a relationship with God or pray until later years of my life.

I also had a brother. He was seven years older than me. If I must be frank, for many years, I did not like him. He treated me so badly. My brother would scare me every chance he got. He tricked me into believing Darth Vader was after me. He was great at imitating Darth Vader's voice. He also used to stick me with compasses. I had little pinholes all over. He would get me in trouble with my dad, and when my dad got upset and wanted to whip me, my brother would say, "Come hide in here," and then drag me to my father while he laughed as I was getting punished. Ugh! Writing this brings back memories, and it gets my blood boiling all over again. This cruelty went on for years!

I once overheard a conversation between him and my mom. My mother said, "Son, you can't keep treating your sister the way you do. It's going to come to a point that your sister will either love or hate you for the rest of your life. Which one do you want her to choose? Now go in your room and think about it."

I clearly remember the day I got fed up with being bullied by my brother. He was 14, and I was 7, and he went to grab the compass. I was mad and said, "No more! You are not going to continue to hurt me. I'm not your personal pin cushion!" I remember praying and asking for help. I don't know where the strength came from, but I PUNCHED him extremely hard in the stomach as he approached me with the compass. I literally knocked the wind out of him. He fell to his knees and looked up at me and said with tears in his eyes, "I guess you're no longer a punk!" My relationship with my brother changed after that. I do not know if it was my mom's conversation with him or because I finally stood up to him. He eventually did become a loving, protective big brother.

I would say among all the other families in our surrounding neighborhood and area, we were privileged. I never saw my parents struggle to put a meal on the table. My parents never needed to decide if the light bill would be paid or if we could afford to go on a school trip. I was fortunate enough to take tap, acrobats, ballet, and I played the piano. Overall, I loved my family, my life and wouldn't have changed a thing.

CHANGE IS INEVITABLE

Change is something we have no control over. The world and most things in the world are forever changing. The seasons change from fall to winter. Technology is forever advancing, and people and their life circumstances go through ups and downs. Change is inevitable. Life in the Altman family was about to change forever.

In 1980, my parents came out of their bedroom and announced that we would have a new addition to the family. Personally, I had mixed feelings. I was the baby of the family and wanted it to stay that way. However, the more I thought about how good it would be to love on a little baby and saw how happy my mother was, the more this new addition started to feel okay.

As the months went by, the more things shifted. The atmosphere in the house was strange. The mood and movement of my parents seemed weird. Though I was a kid, I knew something felt different. However, I knew better than to ask what was going on. As a kid, I was told early on to stay in a kid's place. "Don't mind grown folks' business." I don't really know how to explain it, but I felt something was in the air.

Though the atmosphere in the house was different, little did I know it was about to change. What happened next was a complete shock and I never saw it coming. The day after giving birth to my brother, my mother died. I was only nine years old. Her death was my first experience with feeling broken. The day my mother died, she sat me down and had a conversation with me. She told me how much she loved me and that she was proud of the person I was becoming. In the beginning, I thought nothing of the conversation we were having. I was used to Mom loving on me and building me up because that was who she was. She continued to remind me how much God loved me and that He would always be there for me. Like many times before, she told me to keep God in EVERYTHING I did. She made it so clear because I remember her cupping her hand on my face and saying, "KEEP GOD IN EVERYTHING!" The more she spoke, the more I felt this conversation was different than any other conversation we ever had.

I said, "Mom, why are you talking like this? What's wrong?"

My mom took my hand and said, “Baby, I need you to make me a promise.” My mother asked me to always take care of my dad, my brother, and the baby.

“Why are you saying these things? What’s wrong? Are you hurt? Are you sick? Is it something wrong with you and the baby?” I flooded her with questions that she would not answer. Tears began to fill both our eyes. She gently tried to wipe my tears away, but my tears fell fast and hard!

She said, “If I don’t come back, promise me you will take care of your dad, your brother, and the baby.” With more love overflowing in her eyes and her touch than I’d ever felt before, she said, “I love you, my beautiful daughter. However, I must leave now for the hospital.”

I stood on the porch with streams of tears running down my face. I was asking my mom to come back, not to leave me. I yelled as loud as I could, “Are you coming back?” As the car pulled away, my mom placed her hand on the window and mouthed the words, “I love you!”

At the time, I didn’t know it would be the last time I would see my mother alive. After replaying the scene repeatedly in my head, I believe my mom knew she would not be coming back. I stood on the porch for what seemed forever. I wished with all my might the car would pull back up; and my mom would be there with me once more.

For months after my mom's death, I dreamed of my mom walking through the door, saying, "I'm home!" The reality was, Mom would never walk back through the door. She would never be back with me again. I was hurt and mad at her for leaving me. How was I to go on without her? Not only was I motherless, but I was also confused. I wondered why my mom made me promise to take care of my family, and I could not even take care of myself. How was I going to keep this promise? I was nine!

Shortly after my mom's death, I had to learn how to run and manage a household. I had to learn how to cook, clean, change a baby, warm a bottle, and pay the bills all while going to school. My morning routine was hectic. Most mornings consisted of fixing Dad a breakfast sandwich, some coffee. I also had to remember to take something out to cook for dinner, while getting myself together for school, and any other miscellaneous tasks that presented itself. However, today for whatever reason as I awoke to the sound of my alarm clock, I was overwhelmed and mad as hell! In frustration, I exhaled as I remembered I set my alarm earlier because I had to get up to iron my dad's shirt for work. I was too tired to iron his shirt the night before because I had cooked dinner, washed the dinner dishes, washed, and folded everyone's clothes, and done my homework.

How was I supposed to do this? How would I sustain going to bed late and getting up early almost every day, including the weekends? I was looking forward to summer because that was always my time to do the things I enjoyed. My mother died in

January. I didn't know if I would survive until the summer, but hopefully, then, I could try to do something I wanted.

Summer was close and I was bursting with excitement! Finally, I had three more days before summer vacation. I was looking forward to sleeping in. So many thoughts popped into my head of what activities would fill my summer. Maybe I'd play with my baby dolls, watch a favorite cartoon, or just do nothing. Three, two, one! Summertime! Honestly, the stress of the past few months had reached capacity. I just wanted some time to slow down and grieve. I did not have time to mourn my mother's death because I had to be strong for others while picking up the gauntlet of the woman of the house.

The first day of summer, my dad came into my room and told me I was going on a trip. In some fashion, I was excited because that meant I did not have to get up early to do whatever my dad needed me, or should I say, told me to do. To my dismay, I was going to Cuba, Alabama, to see my grandmother, Lil Mama.

I never enjoyed going down south. The only part of going down south I enjoyed was the food Lil Mama would cook. My mother truly got her cooking skills from her. Alabama was extremely hot. Clothes stuck to places they shouldn't because of the humidity. The bugs were 20 times as big as the ones in the city. The animals were vicious, and, to make matters worse, I had to use an outhouse. Some of you reading this book may understand how horrible using an outhouse is. However, for those who don't, outhouses are dark, stinky, and there's no telling what kind of creature one may encounter. Thankfully, they were in the process of building a bathroom addition to the house, but upon my arrival, it had not yet been completed.

While on the plane, I thought, *why am I heading to Alabama?* When I arrived, Lil Mama had a great spread of food and cakes. This part I truly enjoyed! My grandmother was one of the best cooks ever! Little did I know this great meal was a setup. After dinner, the reason behind my visit became evident.

Lil Mama said, “Shell, did you enjoy your meal?”

“Yes, I did. It was delicious.”

“Good, because tomorrow you are going to learn how to cook the food that was on the table tonight.”

“What!” I said, which I quickly corrected to “Yes, ma’am,” because I didn’t want an unknown object flying my way. No one talked back to Lil Mama.

“Tomorrow morning, we will get up early and begin our first lesson.”

Instantly, the thought that popped into my head was, even here I had to get up early! I hated my life! Clearly, in this lifetime sleeping in wasn’t an option. I went to the bedroom, plopped on the bed, and took turns screaming into the pillow, and hitting it as hard as I could. I truly hated my life!

"Wake up, Shell." I barely opened my eyes to look at the clock. It was 5:30 am. Who wakes up at 5:30 am on a Saturday in the summer to cook? Obviously, ME. Lil Mama said, "Wash up, and I'll meet you in the kitchen by 6. We will cook biscuits for breakfast from scratch." I thought, *I TRULY hate my life and my dad for doing this to me.*

"Okay, baby, time to learn how to be a woman."

I didn't understand why people believed it was time for me to be a woman. I was a 10-year-old kid! I often thought, PLEASE, just let me be a kid.

Over the next three years, my summers were spent down south in Cuba, Alabama. I cried almost every day while there. However, when Lil Mama would see me cry, she would say, "Wipe them tears. You'll appreciate all of this someday."

I prayed for that someday to come, but it didn't seem anywhere in sight. I learned how to snap beans, bake mac and cheese, make the juiciest roast you've ever tasted, bake biscuits, cakes, and pies, etc. My grandmother had a farm with string beans, watermelon, and corn. I had to learn how to pick them from the garden, but interestingly, all these fruits and veggies are now some of my favorites.

I also learned how to sew buttons on clothes, iron a shirt that could stand up on its own, and mop a floor that you could eat off. My grandmother pushed me hard. She'd say, "I got high expectations for you girl, as did your mom."

Lil Mama shared a story with me of my mother praying over me as a baby and stated that I was going to do great things in God's kingdom someday. If great things consisted of knowing how to keep the house and cook a good meal, I was on my way. Being a kid, however, was done. No more playing with dolls or learning how to jump rope. By no choice of my own, it was time to transition from childhood to a woman. FYI, I did one day begin to appreciate my cooking skills. Thanks, Lil Mama!

CHAPTER 2

WHERE I GET MY ROOTS

Roots are an important part of a plant. The roots help to hold a plant in the ground. There are two types of roots – a taproot and a fibrous root. Both the tap and the fibrous roots provide water and nutrients for the plant. The taproot (or primary root) grows deep with thinner roots at the top. Some examples of a taproot are carrots, radishes, and beets. The fibrous root (or secondary root) does not have a main root. It has a bunch of smaller, thinner roots. Some examples of fibrous roots are grass, wheat, and coconut trees. Both tap and fibrous roots can be difficult to uproot. However, taproots are the thicker of the two and would prove to be harder to uproot.

The words spoken over me by my parents would eventually become the roots that shaped my life. Some of the seeds planted by my parents were seeds of life and seeds of death. The Bible says that "Gentle words bring life and health; a deceitful tongue crushes the spirit" (Proverb 15:4). The words spoken over my life would prove to be both positive (life) and negative (death). These words shaped my identity, the choices I would make, and the future words I would speak over myself and my children. Whose report would I believe?

SEEDS PLANTED BY MY MOM

The words my mom spoke over me were words of life. She was an encourager. She motivated me not to give up on dreams, tasks, and myself. She made me believe anything was possible. She was always my biggest cheerleader. I remember when I was learning how to sew dresses for my baby dolls, I would often say, "I can't do this!" I'd get frustrated and want to quit. Mom taught me at an early age the power of my words. "You can do it, but I need you to believe you can do it, and the way you do it is you keep trying. Now keep trying," she'd say while rubbing my back. Thanks to my mom not giving up on me and not letting me give up on myself, I eventually got pretty good at making dresses.

My mom also shared with me the importance of loving God and loving others. "You must love the LORD, your God, with all your heart, all your soul, all your strength, and all your mind; and love your neighbor as yourself" (Luke 10:27, NLT). She not only told me what to do, but she also showed me through her example.

My mother loved the Lord. I often saw her reading her Bible and singing praises to God. It was no question of her love for Jesus. She also loved people. My mom planted seeds of love in me, and everywhere she went. She could be in the grocery store, and just her saying a simple hello to a stranger would ignite a conversation. Conversations that would bloom into laughter or her praying for someone. She had an infectious smile, and it seemed to draw people in.

As a kid, I thought I had the coolest mom ever because everyone wanted to talk to her and be near her. She expressed love in many ways. One example was, how she explained things to me. When I made a bad decision, she'd let me know there was a consequence for every decision I made, but though I had made a bad choice, I was not a bad person. Even though she was scolding me, she had a way of still letting me know I was loved.

I also loved the "for no reason moments" she would have with me. Whether in passing or intentionally, she would make it known she loved me. Not because of anything I had done, but just because of who I was. She would often tell me I was her precious gift. All the moments with my mom would prove to be priceless nuggets of wisdom. I would later discover those nuggets of wisdom my mom shared, referenced something from the Word of God. As mentioned above, Mom loved me "just because." God also loves us. Not because of anything we have done, but because of who He is. He is a God of love.

The first scripture I learned was, "For God so loved the world, that He gave his only begotten Son, that whoever believes in Him shall have everlasting life" (John 3:16). "Believe in God and believe in His Word," she would say. My mom poured so much life and wisdom into me in such a short time. Keep God in EVERYTHING. Though the statement may seem simple, her words were packed with so much goodness. This piece of advice would echo many times, at the right time, over the course of my life.

Mom never said prayer was essential for life, but she didn't have to because I clearly saw it through her example. Praying was something I saw her do. I saw her pray when things were good and when things were bad. She consistently prayed over us and for others. She taught us how to pray over our food and pray before going to bed each night.

My mom was my taproot. Though my mother was in my life for a short time, her imprint would be there forever. Her spoken words, her being a living example, and her outpouring of love is forever rooted in my life. Her expressions of love, truthful words, and powerful prayers would become qualities I would hopefully model.

SEEDS PLANTED BY MY DAD

My dad was a combination of a taproot and a fibrous root. He planted some taproots that grew deep. The fibrous roots he planted were many. Though the roots were small, they spread wide. The fibrous roots were also watered the most. The words my dad spoke over my life varied, like the seasons. When I was younger, he planted words of life. He'd said I love you occasionally, we would laugh, and have father-daughter outings. He was not a man who spoke the words I love you often; he showed love through his actions.

After my mother died, his words became words of death. My father's pain of losing my mom was evident. I cannot imagine the pain he must have felt when my mother died and left behind a

16-year-old son, a 9-year-old daughter, and a 1-day old baby boy. In his defense, I do not believe he had proper time to grieve. He had to stay strong for us while continuing to be a provider. The anger and abandonment he must have felt towards my mom leaving him to care for us kids must have been devastating. Most people have heard the saying, "Hurting people hurt people." I believe that was the case for my father. Though the saying may be true, it does not make it right.

Shortly after my mom died, my dad became verbally abusive. He began to tear me down with his words. The words I love you quickly changed to, "The reason I'm saying these things to you is that I love you and I want you to act right." His tongue towards me became sharper than a two-edged sword.

One day as I was cleaning the kitchen, I accidentally dropped a glass. My father stormed out of his bedroom, came and stood next to me, and said, "How stupid could you be? What the hell is wrong with you?"

I was shocked into stillness. I just stood there and looked at him in disbelief. I could not believe those words came from my father's mouth and were directed at me. Don't get me wrong, my father never had the cleanest choice of words, but they were never directed at me. That night when I went to bed, in the quiet of the night, my dad's words replayed in my mind over and over. I sobbed in my pillow so that no one else would hear me. That night I cried myself to sleep feeling vexed and hurt.

The next morning, I woke up to a throbbing headache. Instantly I hoped the day would be better than the previous night. However, I was the type of person who could never hold on to anger for long. When my parents would discipline (whip) me, I never held on to the anger or hurt I felt after the whipping. I would hop in my dad's lap 10 minutes later as if it never happened. So, this time was no different.

I thought about all the stress my dad must have been under having to do the single-parent thing. I approached the day, saying good morning with a smile, and fixed his daily sandwich and coffee as if nothing ever happened. I even said I love you as he left. Though I was able to let the night before roll off my back, I felt emotionally beaten.

Over the next few weeks, months, and years, my dad's verbal abuse increased. It got to the point that I felt I should change the name on my birth certificate to either "Stupid" or "Good for Nothing." He told me regularly I was worthless and I would not amount to anything. The more I tried to please him, the more I felt defeated. It seemed he took every opportunity to tear down my self-esteem.

He would ask me, "How much bigger are you going to get? If you continue to eat that way, you're going to have to walk through the door sideways." Yes, it's true, I was a plump kid, but I believe eating was how I chose to cope with everything going on. I ate to suppress the pain I felt from having more responsibilities than I could handle and being verbally attacked day after day. I also believe my dependence on food was the way I grieved my mom's death.

I couldn't take much more of it. I was tired of being disrespected, humiliated in front of others, and talked down to. Something needed to change. I had to talk to someone about this. My Aunt Eva (Dad's sister) was one of the people who stepped up and helped in the upbringing of my siblings and me. She took my little brother in and pretty much raised him. I shared with her some of the hurtful names and gestures my father subjected me to. However, I did not get the reaction, comfort, or encouragement I was looking for.

She said, "Baby, often people hurt the ones closest to them. They hurt the one they love most. You are that person for your dad. You are a strong kid. You can handle this!"

I was dumbfounded. My response was, "Well, I'd rather he hate me because if this is love, I don't want it!" As the tears began to fall. I yelled, "Seriously, he's, my father! He is supposed to build me up, not tear me down! He is supposed to be my encourager, my hero, my daddy. He is supposed to love me!" Her statement came as an unwelcome reality check. At that moment, I clearly saw the first man I ever loved felt I was worthless and stupid. WOW!

THE TALK

I was 13 years old when I could no longer take the abuse that was being handed to me daily. I felt it was time to advocate for myself. I had to have a conversation with my dad. However, I had to wait for the right time to approach him. If I didn't do this at the right time, it could backfire and make matters worse. I whispered under my breath, "Help me, Mom, to know when to approach him."

I remember it was on a Saturday early evening. He had cut and watered the grass, cracked open a beer, and said, "Hey, you want to go grab some Church's chicken for dinner?"

I said, "Sure."

He placed the cap back on his beer and said, "Grab the coupons, and I'll meet you at the car."

As we drove to the chicken place, our conversation was pleasant. He was laughing and seemed to be in a good mood. Now was the time. I said, "Hey, Dad, can I ask you a question without you getting upset?"

"Sure, what is it?" As the words started to come out, he said, "Let's wait until we get home before you ask me." I agreed. We got our chicken, and we drove home having another wonderful conversation. Oh, how I missed these times!!

I made our plates and sat at the table. I hoped this conversation would go as well as I wanted it to. I could no longer take being called stupid, worthless, and told I wasn't going to amount to much. I exhaled once, twice, and...then I heard, "What's on your mind?"

"Dad, I need to ask you a question."

"Ok, what's the question?"

"Why do you call me stupid, worthless, and tell me I will never amount to anything? Do you believe I am all those things?"

Silence. My dad got up from the table, walked toward the fridge, and grabbed the beer that he placed in the fridge before we left to get chicken. As he walked back towards the table, he stopped, twisted the top off the beer, took a sip, and then another as he sat back down. Awkward silence... Of course, my mind started racing. I guess it's hard for him to say yes to me face to face... my dad believes I'm stupid... After about two minutes, he said, "I don't believe you're stupid."

"Then why do you say it if you don't believe it?" It was evident this conversation was making him uncomfortable. However, I needed some answers. My dad was never a big conversationalist, but today he needed to try. "Ok, well, let me ask you this. Did Grandma and Grandpa call you insulting, hurtful names?" I chose to say "insulting and hurtful names" because I wanted him to know how being called those names made me feel. His answer to the question was yes.

"Yes, they did."

It seemed my dad was doing what was familiar and what was modeled to him. Just because it is familiar does not make it okay. "How did it make you feel when you were called names by your parents?"

My dad replied, "It hurt."

I looked at him with tears in my eyes and said, "Yeah, Dad, it does."

He lowered his eyes, then his head, and then he popped up like toast from a toaster and said, "I am going to the bathroom."

I cannot say for sure, but I believe he went to the bathroom and cried. I had never seen my dad cry. I do not even remember him crying at my mother's funeral. I believe he grew up around people who told him boys (men) do not cry. I only reference this because I once heard him say to my brother, "Wipe those tears. Boys don't cry!"

Back to the topic at hand. My dad was gone for about five to six minutes. When he returned to the table, I felt it was still important and okay to continue our conversation. I said, "Since you know how being called names made you feel, do you think you could stop calling me names?"

His response was, "I will try."

I immediately got up from the table, walked over to him, grabbed his plate, kissed him on the cheek, and told him I loved him. He said, "I love you, too."

The next three years would prove to be better than the previous years. My dad tried his best to decrease the name-calling. Sometimes he still would slip up and call me a name or say something negative, but he would quickly make eye contact, nod, and walk away. I guess that was his way of acknowledging he was sorry. He never spoke the words I'm sorry, but I guess his gestures had to do.

Instead of rejoicing over "normal things," like feeling loved, passing an exam, or spending time with friends, I rejoiced over not being called stupid. Occasionally my dad would slip up and call me stupid, I did not like the fact I had to accept his random moments of regression. Was this way of living about to be my "new norm?" I did not want it to be, but I found myself celebrating when a week went by without being belittled. However, I walked around daily on eggshells and wondered when the next bomb of insults would drop.

BLENDED FAMILY

My dad remarried when I was eleven or twelve. He married someone who had a daughter a year older than me. Honestly, there was something about my stepmother that didn't sit well in the pit of my stomach. I shared my feelings with my dad. I felt something wasn't right about this woman and I didn't think he should marry her. But my opinion did not hold much weight, and he married her anyway. I will say there were many situations where she tried to destroy my father's relationship with me. She even went as far as trying to get me sent to an out-of-state boarding school. I won't get into much detail, but I will say I believe she was threatened by the relationship I had with my father. I was the one who ran the house for the past two to three years. Plus, the imprint of my mother's presence was still recognizable in the house. I felt she wanted to erase my mom's memory. My stepmother wanted to let me know she was the new woman of the house, and if that took getting rid of me, so be it.

She lied and told my father I was stealing her jewelry, money, and clothing. Did I happen to mention while growing up I was spoiled? I did not have to steal because I didn't want for anything. If there was something I wanted, all I had to do was ask my dad. I truly didn't like having a stepmom, especially this one, and I did not steal the items she accused me of.

I did however enjoy having a big sister. We did things together that I couldn't do with my brother. I enjoyed it when we stayed up late and talked about things only girls talk about. It felt good to have a big sister to look up to. We were like two thieves in the night. As much as I like being around her, I began to witness her do mischievous, yet exciting things.

She had boys over, smoked cigarettes, and would have an occasional drink. Don't get me wrong. I was not as innocent as people thought. I to was curious about boys and wanted to see what the opposite sex was like. It was nice to talk with someone who understood my feelings. She knew more than I did, but I was not afraid to try some of the things offered.

At the age of 15, I felt I had learned all the things a woman of the house was supposed to learn. I had become proficient at doing laundry, cooking, and cleaning. I wanted to know what else women did, what other fun things were out there for us "women". I wanted to start living life on my own accord.

I began pushing the boundaries my dad set in place for me. I wanted to see how far I could stretch the boundary line. I started cutting a couple of classes here and there. When the school called to report my absence, I'd always have a good excuse on why he received the call. He believed my explanation every time. Then I began to test the house rules. I extended my curfew time little by little. My dad did not seem to notice me stretching the limits. I also got to know my dad's and stepmother's schedule better than I knew my own. I figured out by watching others how to have naughty fun and not get caught. It was time to do things MY way!

Doing things my way meant I had to pursue a like-minded crowd. People I could discuss my mischievous behaviors with, without judgment. It was time to branch out to find my own group to hang out with and share experiences with. I was the first to experience everything. I was the first to get liquor to share, cigarettes to smoke, and to have the first kiss. It was exciting to be the center of attention and have all eyes on me. My circle of friends looked forward to our weekend tell-all sessions. Most times, it was me telling all.

When I got with my sister and her friends, I could always count on someone sharing a good juicy story. A story that would make my adventures seem small. We were not in competition, but it made for good conversation to discuss our escapades. My sister seemed to be having more adventures than I. However, she always seemed to get caught. She was either getting picked up for curfew or being caught in a lie. On the surface, my sister seemed to be the troublemaker and I the innocent one, but I wasn't as innocent as I looked. I credit my innocent façade to watching and studying my sister in action. I learned what not to do from her mistakes. Over time she perfected her craft. She became slick as oil. Her days of getting caught were becoming few and far between. She was the best teacher ever. Because of her, I learned to fly below the radar. I always kept an eye on her to see what my next "first" would be. Over the next few months, I discovered being first wasn't everything it was cracked up to be.

At age 16 I was the first to announce I was pregnant. I remember the days leading up to telling my parents that I, the "innocent one," was going to have a baby. I was terrified! I purchased so many pregnancy tests that I should have purchased stock in the company. I continued to take tests in hopes one of them would read negative. The test continued to read positive. I was pregnant!

The first person I told was my best friend. We cried together, all while trying to come up with a plan to make this go away. The next person I told was the father. He quickly said, "It's not mine." Then in the next breath, he said, "Have an abortion." I could have filled up a swimming pool with my tears. I wanted his support, not denial and rejection of the truth. Before I knew it, a month or more had passed, and I needed to tell my parents. The last conversation I had before telling my parents was with my sister. She looked surprised yet appeared to have a sense of relief on her face.

"Why are you looking at me that way?" I asked.

She said, "Just bite the bullet and tell them." That's easy for you to say, I thought! She said, "Trust me, I got your back." I didn't understand what she could do to make this process any easier except stand in between my dad and me. I knew he was going to be furious but, more than anything, disappointed. I could handle furious, but him being disappointed was another level. Here's how it went.

"Hey, guys, I need to let you know I am pregnant." Silence. Then the dam broke open! The floodgates of derogatory words began to fill the air. Then I heard my stepmom say, "Hmm, you thought my daughter was the mischievous one, and it's YOUR daughter who is pregnant!" The only thing I could think of was how I could escape. I remember I closed my eyes as if that would silence the words being thrown my way.

And then, in the distance, I heard, "Save some of that anger for me, too." My sister, in her own way, absolutely had my back. She announced, "I am pregnant, too!"

My parents were speechless. I was also shocked by her news and, at the same time, relieved to not be in this whirlwind alone. "Get out of our faces. We do not want to look at you two right now!" However, before we could honor their request, they stormed to their bedroom and slammed the door. The next nine months were going to be interesting.

In the beginning, my pregnancy was a struggle. The struggles were not related to the pregnancy itself. The battle was due to the obvious tension between my dad and me. I am thankful the saying if looks could kill is not true, because based on the looks I received whenever I was in my dad's presence, I would have been dead. My father looked at me with pure disgust. Plus, the insults that came from his mouth were even worse. It got to the point that my father told me he did not want to see my face anymore. He told me I had to get out! Where was I going to go? I was 16, with no job, no money, and no idea how to care for this baby that I was carrying inside my belly. I hoped my father was just really, really upset, and by morning he would have changed his mind.

No such luck. My father had not changed his mind. He told me I had a couple of days to find somewhere else to live. Wow! All I could do was cry! After crying for an hour or so, I knew I needed to figure out my next steps. The next couple of days were going to be rough. My mental state was pushed to the limit. Should I have this baby, or should I have an abortion?

I researched being a teen mother, abortions, and adoption. It seemed the more research I did, the more confused I became. The one thing I did decide was having an abortion was not an option. However, that day I did make an appointment to discuss giving the baby up for adoption. After making an appointment, the next task for the day was deciding where I would live. Maybe I can spend a couple of nights at a friend's house. Spending the night with friends did not get the response I thought.

Remember, I was the first person in my group to have the "first" life experiences. Well, I was also the first-person viewed as a "bad influence." Considering I was the first to get pregnant, many, if not most, of my friends' parents did not want me hanging around. I believe the parents thought I might influence my friends to follow in my footsteps.

Honestly, my advice was just the opposite. I told everyone who would listen not to get pregnant. I shared how the consequences of my choices were not worth all the disappointment and broken relationships I had to deal with. I had to find another place to stay. I had no idea of where I was going. I hoped I would have more luck the next day.

I woke up the next morning, determined to find a place to live. My first call was back to the adoption agency. I asked if you got paid to give your baby up for adoption. I quickly heard a sharp "no!" from the person who answered the phone. I was clueless, alone, and frightened. I did not know I shouldn't have asked the question. I did not know the process of adoption, but I was desperate, and I needed help and money for a place to live. The familiar feeling of abandonment was surfacing once more. I had not been in this place of feeling lost and abandoned since my mother's death. Even when my dad was upset with me, he still provided for my basic needs. However, this time was different, and I was on my own.

I grabbed the telephone book and looked up pregnant teens. I found a school for pregnant moms. I called to see what the program was about. I wondered if it was a boarding school. I needed somewhere I could call home, at least for the moment. The school did not house you, but it provided the amenities needed to continue my education while pregnant. However, I still needed a place to lay my head. I had to trust somehow, it would all work out.

Things were not working out as I had hoped. My dad made it clear he did not want me in his house. If I was in the room, he quickly exited. The only conversation I had with him during that time was him asking me where I was moving to. I did not know where I was going, but I decided that maternity school was a good option. Maybe if I shared this information with my dad, he would soften his heart and let me stay. I shared my plans of attending maternity school. My dad quickly asked was it a boarding school. I replied, no. He said, "Well, you still need to find somewhere to stay. I don't want you living here!"

I quickly snapped back, "I'm trying!" I thought to myself, you don't want me here. I get it! However, I'm so tired of hearing the same thing repeatedly. I understand I screwed up, and I already feel ashamed. I don't need my dad constantly ragging me. To attend this school, I needed my dad to transfer me from one school to the other. Anything related to helping me during this pregnancy was a hindrance to him. I was at the end of my rope.

Later that night, I overheard a conversation my dad was having with my aunt. It was the same aunt that was helping raise my brother. I heard my dad say, "Yes, I am putting her out! She's an embarrassment." Everything was starting to make sense. My dad never liked being embarrassed. Honestly, no one does, but my pregnancy not only made him angry to the extreme but also embarrassed him. Growing up, he told us not to be loud in the stores or do anything that would draw negative attention. I never thought about how my being pregnant made him feel. I knew he was angry, hurt, and disappointed without question, but I never thought about him being embarrassed.

Shortly, after my dad finished talking to my aunt, I decided to call her. I expressed my concerns about not having a place to stay and the thought of giving the baby up for adoption. The tears began to fall again. One thing I noticed right away was how my emotions were all over the place. Crying became a natural occurrence. My aunt told me to stop crying and trust everything would work out. I shared the information about the maternity school and told her I needed to be transferred. She told me not to worry about the details of how I would get transferred. She would handle everything.

She then said, “You know I do not have much room, but you are welcome to sleep on my couch.” I had a sigh of relief. Thank God!

That night I began to pack my clothes. I packed about two weeks’ worth and hoped my dad would change his mind and let me come back home. By early afternoon the next day, my aunt was there exactly when she said she would be.

My aunt was always there for me. Once back at her house, we chatted for a while. I asked if she wanted me to make us sandwiches for lunch. I felt as if I should lighten some of her load because she had lightened mine. At that moment, I was so thankful for her. I felt loved. She was one person who kept me encouraged. Though she expressed her disappointment that I was pregnant, in the same breath, she told me she loved me no matter what. It was just what I needed to hear. If she had not let me stay with her, I do not know where I would have gone. The day went fast. Though I did not do much, I was very emotionally and physically tired.

The next morning, I peeled myself off the hot couch covered with plastic. I had an appointment with the adoption agency. Not only were my hormones all over the place, but I also had to decide if adoption was the way to go. I felt like a yoyo on a string. However, I went to the appointment with an open mind. One of the things I liked about the organization was that they did not make me feel pressured to decide if I would give this baby up for adoption. The organization provided plenty of information and answered all my questions. They told me to take my time with my decision.

This was a big decision, and so much was going on in my head. This was not a decision I could make on the spot. Therefore, I told them I needed to think about this for a few weeks. However, before leaving, I did make a follow-up appointment for four weeks. How will I decide?

Once I was back at my aunt's house, I asked her opinion. She told me to pray about it. I decided to make a pros and cons list. The pros outweighed the cons. Bottom line, I did not have the means to take care of a baby. I hoped the upcoming weeks would provide the answer I needed.

Four weeks went by fast. As I awoke, I felt a quiver in my belly. I froze like a deer caught in headlights. Did I feel what I think I did? I laid as still as I could, closed my eyes, put one hand on my belly, and waited. Nothing. I'm trippin', I thought to myself. It's too early to feel this baby moving. If I must be honest, I had not been to a doctor, and I did not know how far along I was.

I began getting ready for the day. I took a shower, got dressed, and made breakfast. As I went to sit down, I felt another quiver and another. Again, I quickly put my hand on my belly and waited. I felt my baby move! Immediately, I knew the answer to the question that had been haunting me for a month. I would not be giving my baby up for adoption. At that moment, I was instantly in love with this little one growing inside my belly.

My pregnancy was beginning to be great. My hair grew long, my skin glowed, and I didn't have much morning sickness. Maternity school was also going well. I was learning the skills needed to care for my child. Plus, close to the end of my fifth month, my dad came to my aunt's house and told me I could come home. He helped me get everything that was needed to provide for my son and treated me better. However, I still felt an emptiness. I missed my mom so much during this time. I am sure she would have had some good advice for me.

Being in labor was not what I expected. I do not know what I expected labor to be, but it wasn't being surrounded by a bunch of screaming women. Being at the county hospital didn't provide much privacy. I heard the other moms screaming in pain, and I wanted out! I asked the nurse if I could go to the bathroom, but instead, I hopped on the elevator and planned my escape. I tried to leave the hospital wearing a hospital gown, an IV in my hand, and a pole to follow.

After being caught by the security guard, I was taken back to the maternity floor and put on a 1:1 watch. This baby was coming no matter how fearful I was. I had no choice but to go through the process. I was 17 when I birth a healthy 8lb 14oz curly-head baby boy. Things seemed to be okay.

Over the next three years, I had many transitions, but life was good. At 18, my dad got me a new car off the showroom floor, and I was able to move into my own house. My dad paid my car note, insurance, and all the bills for the house for the first five years. Dad also spoiled his first grandchild. Life as I knew it was amazing! At 19, I had another baby. This time I had a beautiful bald-head, gray-eyed little girl. She was 6lbs 14ozs.

SPOKEN WORDS OVER MY CHILDREN

Due to growing up most of my life with some form of verbal abuse, I knew the negative impact and hurt carelessly spoken words could cause. I knew how it felt to be told day after day that I was not good enough. My dad's verbal aggressions planted seeds of doubt, hopelessness, and low self-esteem. His words would leave wounds that would take many years to heal. I vowed long before I had kids, I would never make them feel how my dad made me feel growing up. I would not tear them down. I would build them up and let them know they were loved and valued.

Each one of my children was a gift from God. I had a surprise gift at the age of 27. A gorgeous 6lbs 3oz baby girl. Though I was clueless about how to raise my children, I knew I had to give them back to God because there was no better place for them to be than in His hands. I will be the first to admit, the process of raising my children was filled with plenty of mistakes, emotions, uncertainties, joys, and sorrows. I wanted to provide the best life possible for them. However, I fell short many days.

Before the madness, my children were my world. I showed up for them as a mom should. I made sure all their basic needs were met, we had exciting family outings, and I was the mom at the school functions who unapologetically screamed loudly in the stand for her kids. I also believed in disciplining them. Proverbs 22:6 says, "Train up a child in the way he should go; even when he is old, he will not depart from it". I believe I came out of the womb an affectionate person. Physical touch and quality time are tied for my love language. If any of my children were asked about my affectionate behaviors, I'm sure they would say it was extreme. Every chance I got I was rubbing their arm, hugging them, and loving on them. I wanted them to know there was no question I loved them. I tried my best to speak words of life over them. I told them they were smart, capable of much, and I believed in them.

As my addiction increased, my children's needs got lost in the fog of the madness. My presence in their lives slowly decreased. Me showing up for them lessened the deeper engulfed I became in my dependence on drugs. Meeting their basic needs shifted to fulfilling my need for the next high. I was no longer the mom who attended my children's events and cheered them on. The strong personal bond we shared became strained. I became a mom of broken promises. I became unreliable and the mother my children had to hide anything of value from. I became the mother they could no longer recognize nor trust. I had become the parent that I vowed I would never become. Intergenerational abuse is when ill-treatment experienced during childhood is repeated by a child as they get older within their own adult family (Julie Nguyen, Hilary Jacob Hindel. Mindbodygreen).

The cycle of neglect had come full circle three generations. I passed down to my children some of the same hurtful feelings I dreaded as a child. Though I did not tear them down verbally, I had physically and emotionally neglected them. My cravings were often more powerful than the need to do the right thing.

In the smog of the madness, it never crossed my mind that every decision I made impacted the lives of my children. I have had lots of guilt about conversations I should have had with them, times I should have been there just because, and those missed moments of providing those foundational principles they needed for life. I want to take the time to apologize again to my children for not being the mother they needed me to be during certain times in their lives. I am sorry I selfishly placed my needs above you and your needs. I trust God that the cycle of neglect ends with you. I pray God heals you everywhere I've hurt you. I am thankful to God that He cared for you, loved you, and surrounded you with people of support when I didn't. I give all praises to God for His extended grace while keeping you under His mighty wing of protection.

CHAPTER 3

INTRODUCTION TO MADNESS

Around my 20th birthday, I had a party that would change my life forever. My sister offered me a gift that would control my life, destroy valued relationships, and take me to a place of madness. That gift was a line of cocaine. That line of cocaine was the gateway to other drugs. I began to smoke weed, smoke crack, and an occasional happy stick. Alcohol was also heavily present. However, crack was my drug of choice.

When I first started getting high, I thought I could handle it. I said, "I'm not like "those other people" who were too weak. I was stronger, more disciplined, and I would prove to be better than the rest. Little did I know, I had crossed over to befriending pride and judgment. Throwing stones at others made me blind to the fact I was no better than anyone else, nor was I invincible.

My addiction started out as a social thing. I was able to get high on occasion with friends and think nothing about it for weeks. My transition from social use to regular use became clear when I started meeting with a certain group of people on the same day of the week. There were also times I would use by myself. I hid my addiction very well. I could be hanging out with family and be high as a kite, and no one was the wiser. I was a "functional" addict for years. I could go to work and get through the day without the thought of getting high.

I knew I was dependent on drugs when I started missing work. Before my addiction, I had a strong work ethic. I was never late for my shifts, and I did not call in. My dad instilled in us the importance of doing your job well. No mediocre job performance allowed! I was taught to arrive at work in enough time to sit down, have a cup of coffee, and clear my head for the task ahead. However, I found myself running in the door more often to punch in on time. I began justifying my using. I felt it was okay to use if I had a rough day at work or out of boredom. Eventually, it got to the point that I would think about using during work.

I would watch the clock anticipating the end of my shift. I used to work the morning shift, but I switched to the second shift after using a year or so. I enjoyed working second shift because it accommodated my schedule of getting high. I got off at 11 pm, got high until 4 or 5 am, slept until 1:45 pm or so, and back to work I went. At least there were some nights I did not indulge. In my eyes, I was doing fine. I did not realize my life was on a downward spiral.

Down the rabbit hole, I went. I knew I was an addict when I would call off work on a regular basis. Then I would drop my kids off as if I were going to work and get high the entire eight hours. My cravings became bad. I would even dream about getting high.

In between paydays, I would lie to my family to get money. The more I got high, the more I wanted to.

I began to develop a physical and psychological dependence. I started having withdrawals when I had not used drugs for at least three days. I would experience moodiness, anger, and stomach cramps. In order not to feel this pain, I would use. I was officially on the road to madness.

In this stage of my addiction is when my family started noticing something about me was different. When I would be invited to family functions out of selfishness I would decline. I preferred doing what I enjoy versus spending quality time with them. They'd asked me if I was okay, and I would lie and say, "I just don't feel good." The thing about life is what is done in the dark will eventually come to light. The road of madness I was about to travel would take me places I never imagined.

STEALING

I was traveling a road that was leading me to destruction. I was so focused on getting high I was not aware that I was out of control. All my moral values had gone out the window. Respect for myself and others, being honest, and being compassionate had left the building.

I eventually quit my job, because I wanted to get high more than punching a time clock. I worked in healthcare and my job was to provide quality care. However, my job performance had suffered tremendously due to my addiction. I would lie to my boss about why my job performance was lacking. It was getting too hard to keep up the façade. Seems like I would have thought it be better to keep my job to support my habit, but rational thinking had disappeared.

After quitting my job, I continued to tell my family I was working. I asked family and friends to borrow money until my next check, but the next check never came. The lies I told to my loved ones were increasing, the stories were forever changing, and the lies were getting harder to keep track of. Ultimately, I had exhausted my resources of borrowing money and begging so much that people turned the other way when they saw me coming. I began looking for more creative ways to support my habit.

My first choice was to steal anything I could either sell or trade for drugs. That worked well for a while, but I had either stolen everything worth value from everyone possible, or people got wise and did not leave anything out worth stealing. My stealing was so bad my father put a padlock on his bedroom door. I had to figure out a new way to support my habit.

RELATIONSHIPS

My drug addiction wreaked havoc on everything that once was good, including my relationships. Intervention day: I walked in the house after being on a drug binge for about three days, and there was a house full of people sitting in the kitchen – my kids, father, aunt, brother, and my pastor. I thought nothing of it, and I walked right past them. All I wanted was to climb in the bed and crash. I was told to come sit down. I knew instantly that the meeting at the kitchen table was orchestrated on my behalf. I let them know through my gestures that I was annoyed and not interested in talking about "how Michele is screwing up her life."

My pastor started the conversation of why they were all gathered there. Each person had their time to speak. Two out of three of my children were present. My son was about 14 or 15. My oldest daughter had to be about 12 or 13. I was presented with the opportunity to go to rehab. The echoing words of "please go get some help" were partnered with tears. Personally, I did not see this as an act of love; I felt attacked.

I told them, "I'm not going to anyone's damn rehab!" I got up from the table, went to my room, grabbed some clothes and other random items, and quickly opened the fridge, took a couple packs of Buddig lunch meat, and back out the door I went. No intervention for me today!

I had many setbacks in my relationship with my father, but I could always count on him to help. Though his support may have been slow coming and sometimes harsh, he was there. Once I was engulfed in the madness, and the offers of rehab were turned down several times, my dad had no choice but to extend a hand of tough love.

There were many times I could not feed myself, take care of myself, or even love myself, and I needed someone's support. However, unless I agreed to my family's terms and conditions, everyone was instructed not to give me anything but a meal. Because I was noncompliant, I had to move out of the house I once lived in and move back in with my dad. It got to the point I was not able to pay my bills or keep up with the maintenance anymore. Plus, I was using it as a drug flop house – meaning I let people come get high and crash. I let drug dealers crash there to make their sales. It was the next level of how I supported my habit. People used my house to get high, and I got drugs. I was so upset about having to move back in with my dad, but clearly not enough to turn my life around. Plus, my dad felt this was a way of keeping me close. He felt if he could monitor my goings and comings and put me on a curfew, I would not get high.

My dad told me how stupid I was to mess up my life by doing drugs. I believe his heart was in the right place. He just had a crappy way of showing it. He loved me the best he knew how. The older I got, the less I heard I love you. That was unless I said it first, and even then, it was dry.

Though my dad didn't express his love for me much anymore, I was given the opportunity to witness my dad still loved me. He loved me just as much as he did when I was a little girl climbing into his lap. One late night as I was sneaking in the house, I overheard and saw him praying for me. I heard him say, "Lord, please save my daughter! Do not let the drugs or the streets kill her. I love her. Help her. Please!" This was the only time I ever witnessed my father crying.

My relationship with my two oldest children also became strained. In my madness, I would test their love for me on many occasions. I stole from them, lied, and wasn't present most days. One good thing I can say I instilled into my children during my madness was the importance of getting an education and not falling victim to their circumstances. I told them to go to school. I told them not to be a statistic. Do not let it be said they were not able to be successful because their mom was a crackhead. Let it be said they chose to be successful because they did not want to follow the path of their mom.

Many times, during my son's high school years, he came and grabbed me off the streets, protected me from dangerous situations, and covered me in prayer. One day as my son was coming home from school, he noticed me through the window of the city bus. He got off the bus, grabbed my arm, and said, "Woman, you look a hot mess and you're coming home! I had not been home in a couple of days. He was the person who saw me at my worst during my days of madness. I know it hurt him to see me this way, but he kept a straight face as if it didn't.

Honestly, I feel he wanted and needed to be strong for his sisters and for me. No matter who said negative things about me, he would say, "Do not talk about my mom. God is going to deliver her!" I do not know, nor do I care, what was said behind closed doors, but what I do know is that from my perspective, my son never gave up on me. He told me, "Woman, you got to get better, and I know you can!"

I believe my addiction hurt and affected all my children differently. However, my middle child's hurt, and disappointment was visible. I was not there for many of the special moments in her life. I know I hurt her to the core. She loved me dearly, and I abused and took advantage of that many times. I lied to her to get what I wanted, stole precious items, and even broke her favorite piggy bank that she'd had for years to support my habit. Her process and healing time would be longer than the rest.

One weekend, my daughter came home from college to visit, and out of the blue, she said, "I need some space. I need time to process everything you did. I need time to heal." I was asked not to contact her. She did not want me to call her, text her, or write her. She further explained she was not trying to hurt me. She needed to take this time for her own well-being.

Before leaving to go back to school, she said, "I love you. Please respect my wishes, and I will contact you when I am ready." I did not hear from her for about three months. That was one of the toughest seasons of my life. Thankfully, I can say once she reached back out to me, we were able to rebuild our relationship. Our relationship is now stronger than it was before.

My youngest daughter was too young to know that her mom was a trainwreck. I am thankful for all the people that sheltered her during her early years. However, during her preteen years, she witnessed some of the madness I was in. She recalls me not being home much, and when I did come home, it was brief. I tried to cover up my absence by buying her stuff. Sad to think I was so lost that I thought a few bags of chips would supplement spending quality time with her. Due to my absence, she pretty much did what she wanted when she wanted. In later years I found out how much my absence impacted her. She was a victim of abuse that would have been prevented if I had not been on drugs. Due to my absence and lack of supervision, she was raped. She was forced to experience something no one, especially an innocent child should.

PROSTITUTION

The first day I decided to prostitute myself for drugs was after I had been getting high with a female companion and the drugs were gone. She was into prostitution and not ashamed of it. She often talked about how quick and easy it was. In previous times when she would bring it up in conversation, I'd say," More power to you girl, I'll never prostitute myself." But I also was the one who said I was stronger than "other people" and I would never become an addict. "Never say "never" about anything, because if you do, life has a way of humbling you" -Mike Colter.

In this addiction, I quickly learned not to be so quick to say what I would not do because no sooner than I said it, I was doing it. Nevertheless, here I was in this situation. I will call this companion Sara. Sara said, "All we have to do is go over this guy's house and party with him and his friend. They will have everything we needed. Smokes, liquor, and drugs." I was terrified, but as I said earlier, my morals were gone. The desire for drugs was greater than my moral values.

At this point in my addiction, the desire for drugs had become greater than my relationships with family and friends, and even at times, greater than the concern for my own safety. The first couple of times, I cried from the guilt and shame of who I had become and what I was doing to support my habit. The deeper in darkness and despair I went, the more I lost myself. I risked my life every time I got in the car with strangers.

Prostitution became my new 9 to 5. A vicious cycle began. The more I did drugs, the more I needed to put myself in compromising situations; the more I prostituted myself. I am thankful to be able to say that I was safe when it came to doing my business. I made sure I utilized the resources provided within the community that handed out condoms. If I were going to shame myself day in and day out, I would protect myself from disease.

LIFE ON THE STREETS

Life on the streets of Chicago was dangerous. It was madness, but madness was becoming my norm. I was in a state of hopelessness and was making extremely poor choices. I called my drug addiction madness because of a comment I made one day after a long binge and a traumatic experience. I had gotten beat up for owing a drug dealer money. I remember I plopped in the bed and started to reflect on my life. I said aloud, “Girl, this world you’re living in is pure madness!” The world of madness was a world I created for myself, but the sad thing is I didn’t know how I got there so fast.

I was living a chaotic life. My newfound circle was running with drug dealers, thieves, and prostitutes. As a child, I never dreamt my life would be this way. I abandoned a stable life and a family that loved and supported me for a detestable life on drugs. Drugs became my life. I lived out in the streets more than I was at home. However, I believe being in the streets (the wilderness) is where I began to realize how far I had fallen from reality, everyone, and everything that was once important to me. This world of madness is where I would see how God carried, protected, and loved me. I got to the point that I didn’t even love myself. It was disgusting to see who I had become and the means I would stoop to satisfy my habit. During this time, I would repeatedly witness God’s love, mercy, and grace towards me.

I grew up on the South Side of Chicago, in the Roseland community. It was known as the “wild, wild hundreds.” It would prove to live up to its name. I can attest to seven visible times God saved me out there on those streets. One night I got in a car with a man and little did I know, he planned to kill me. The details of what led up to that point are not important, but what I will say is, what came from his mouth let me know he planned on ending my life.

We were in a wooded area, it was dark, and no one was around. He asked me if I knew what today was? Before I could respond, he said, "This is the day you die!" I quickly tried to open the door, only to get my fingers slashed by the sharpened door lock. The car had door locks that you pulled up or pushed down, not automatic locks. He had removed the lock covers and sharpened them. The door handle was also missing and sharpened. Once someone was in, there was no getting out unless he opened the door.

I looked into his eyes. They were dark and evil. I was terrified! Before I knew it, a gun was to my head. I remember saying aloud, "Lord, don't let me die this way!" My heart was beating so fast! Shortly after calling out to Jesus, I remember the man getting nervous. He began talking to himself, words I could not quite understand. He seemed discombobulated. "JESUS, help me!"

Though I could not make out most of the words he said, I was able to hear him say, as he was shaking his head "No, not this way, too messy." When he said that, it led me to believe the experience that was occurring was new for both of us. His confusion increased, as did his frustration. However, the frustration was with himself. I thought to myself, *was this the first time he was doing this?* It seemed he was trying to figure out the right way to accomplish his goal of killing me. He continued to mumble to himself. He quickly got out of the car, ran to open my door, and said to me, "You don't know how lucky you are today, but soon you will. RUN!"

I ran as fast as I could! About two or three weeks later, there was a buzz on the streets for prostitutes to be careful. Prostitutes were being found dead in abandoned buildings in my neighborhood. When I heard this, my heart instantly dropped to my stomach. The replay of what happened to me weeks prior was back with vengeance. *You don't know how lucky you are today, but soon you will. RUN!* OMG, I was in the car with this man, the man-killing my friends!

Here is a copy of the article:

ROSELAND FEARS A SERIAL KILLER

Sabrina L. Miller and Noreen S. Ahmed-Ullah, Tribune Staff Writers. Tribune staff writers Terry Wilson, Mickey Ciokajlo and Noah Isackson contributed to this report.

CHICAGO TRIBUNE

For the sixth time in two months, police Tuesday discovered the decomposed body of a woman in an abandoned building in the Greater Roseland community on Chicago's South Side, heightening fears among residents that a serial killer could be on the loose.

The woman, who police have not identified, died of multiple stab wounds and blunt head trauma, according to the Cook County medical examiner's office.

All the victims are African American, all were found in abandoned buildings in or near Roseland, and all suffered some combination of blunt head trauma, strangling, or stabbing. Police believe some of the women engaged in "high-risk" lifestyles, such as prostitution and substance abuse, and that they were lured to their deaths with drugs.

Authorities are investigating whether the slayings are linked, but they have a suspect in custody, Geoffrey T. Griffin, who police say has admitted committing the first of the six slayings and has been charged with first-degree murder. Police are awaiting results of DNA tests on all of the victims to determine whether there is a connection between the crimes.

But the slayings have evoked an eerie reminder of the fear and anger that rippled through the Englewood neighborhood after a rash of killings between 1995 and 1999 of women, whose bodies, like those in Roseland, were found in abandoned buildings.

Police were sharply criticized by Englewood residents for being slow to warn of the dangers facing the community. In the Roseland slayings, however, authorities appear to have acted quickly to spread word.

Police stumbled upon the latest Roseland victim early Tuesday as they searched a building in the 11000 block of South Edbrooke Avenue on an unrelated criminal investigation.

Residents had earlier complained of a foul odor coming from the building but dismissed it as a dead animal.

Police say Griffin has been linked by forensic evidence to the first victim, Angela Jones, whose body was found May 12.

Griffin, who was released from the Illinois River Correctional Center in Downstate Canton in March, after serving a year for aggravated battery with intent to do great bodily harm to a Roseland woman, has been in custody in connection with the Jones slaying since June 17. Police say he gave a videotaped statement admitting his role in the killing but has not implicated himself in any of the other slayings.

While police continue to investigate Griffin, 29, some Roseland-area residents say they are angry and frustrated by the proliferation of abandoned buildings in their community. Some said if police and city officials had done more to secure the buildings or demolish them altogether, the killings might not have happened.

"This could have been prevented, I do believe," said Clee Lowe, chairman of the Developing Communities Project, a church-based community-activist group that has pressured the city to address the abandoned building problem.

"Something should have been going all the time. It has taken six people who have lost their lives to get some attention," he said.

But City Building Commissioner Mary Richardson Lowry said Tuesday that the city has cracked down on owners of abandoned buildings. Unlike in the Englewood killings, where women were lured to abandoned buildings that were not secure and in grave disrepair, all of the buildings except one in the Roseland slayings were boarded up.

The building where Tuesday's victim was found was boarded, and the property manager, Allen Harris, said he had been there as recently as Saturday to check the locks and boards. He said he smelled a foul odor then but dismissed it, thinking that there was "a dead cat under the porch."

"If someone is determined to enter a structure, it is virtually impossible to keep them out," Lowry said.

The Building Department has identified about 125 abandoned buildings in Greater Roseland, "A significant figure in an otherwise stable community," Lowry said.

Ald. Anthony Beale (9th) said he blames the large number of abandoned buildings in Roseland on the fact that the neighborhood has "the highest number of foreclosures in the United States."

When you have a high number of foreclosures, the abandonment rate is very high," he said.

In an attempt to reduce the dangers posed by vacant buildings, the City Council in May created the Vacant Buildings Registration Program, requiring building owners to register abandoned buildings with the city, maintain liability insurance on the structures, and ensure that they are secure. Violators can be fined $200 to $1,000 a day, Lowry said.

"You do get into some red tape when it comes to these buildings. The city can't just come in and board up a building," Beale said. "We are trying to hold the owners accountable for their buildings."

As area police conducted a sweep of more abandoned buildings Tuesday, Roseland neighborhood residents, like their Englewood counterparts in recent years, said they were fearful a serial killer could be targeting neighborhood women.

"My boyfriend won't let me go anywhere unless I'm in his car or he's with me," said Alicia Moore, 25, a lifelong Roseland resident.

Moore, whose boyfriend lives on the block where Tuesday's victim was found, said she also fears for the safety of her mother, who rides a CTA bus home late at night and walks home alone from the bus stop.

"This is a heinous crime. Am I scared? Of course, I am," Moore said.

Despite Griffin's alleged confession to one of the Roseland slayings, some neighborhood residents were as cautious as police about linking him to all of the crimes—even though they bore similarities to the battery for which he served prison time.

According to court documents related to Griffin's 1999 guilty plea, Griffin was walking in an alley early last year when he approached a woman, asked her if she was dating anyone, and then went into an abandoned building to smoke crack with her. Thinking the victim stole money from him, Griffin began to beat her, striking her with a beer bottle and a stick and burning her face with a cigarette lighter. Then he choked her until she passed out. She regained consciousness after he left and sought help.

The victim's mother, Elaine Sharp, said her daughter, who was 26 years old at the time of the attack, had "a history of drug abuse and soliciting."

Sharp was angry that Griffin had been released from prison. "They had him," Sharp said, "and they let him go."

Relatives of Griffin said they don't believe police had the right man in custody for the Jones slaying. Griffin's older sister, Kathryn, said her brother was an easy target because of his aggravated battery conviction. She said she sent a lawyer to see her brother in jail, and the lawyer alleged that Griffin said he was beaten into confessing.

Calumet Area Sgt. Jim Boylan denied any force was used to obtain the confession, noting that Griffin's statement was videotaped.

Kathryn Griffin said her brother has worked two jobs, at McDonald's and Burger King in south suburban Olympia Fields, since his release from prison. She said he had previously been through rehabilitation for cocaine addiction.

"I just don't believe my brother is capable of doing this. If he did these crimes, he needs to be punished," she said. "I don't believe he's a serial killer."

Relatives and friends of the fifth victim, Beverly Burns, whose body was found Thursday, focused on her life at a Tuesday service, rather than the tragic way she died.

More than 100 people filled a chapel at Gatling's funeral home for Burns, 39, nicknamed "Topsy."

"Yes, she was a substance abuser, but if you're talking about a heart, she had a great heart," said Burns' niece, Shonda Wilson.

> Rev. Robert McGee Sr., who eulogized Burns, added, "Whoever has done what they've done is going to pay the price."[1]

Reading this article always brings a wide array of emotions. I am instantly taken back to the moment I was in the car fearing for my life. I remember how it felt to cut my finger on the sharpen door locks, and I remember the smell that was present in the car. Yet, today as I type, more than anything I am overwhelmed with gratefulness. I do not dismiss anyone that lost their lives during this tragedy. However, I can't help but think the names of the deceased women in this article could have been me. But God! I must stop and give honor and praise to God for saving me. Lord, thank You for protecting me. Thank You for keeping me from death. I would not be here, if not for your grace! "I will give thanks to you, LORD, with all my heart; I will tell of all your wonderful deeds" (Psalm. 9:1, NIV).

I do not know for certain if I was his first intended victim or if he was trying to change his methods. What I do know is my life was spared! Over the next couple of months, I knew four of the six women that would die at the hands of this man. But God had another plan for me and for that I am thankful.

---

1. Sabrina L. Miller and Noreen S. Ahmed-Ullah, Tribune Staff Writers. Tribune staff writers Terry Wilson, Mickey Ciokajlo, Noah Isackson. "Roseland Fears a Serial Killer." https://www.chicagotribune.com/news, Chicago Tribune, Jun 28, 2000, https://www.chicagotribune.com/news/ct-xpm-2000-06-28-0006280270-story.html

Though this severe thing happened to me, and the experience should have scared me straight, I couldn't stop my destructive behaviors. I had fallen so deep into the pit of despair; I could no longer see the light. Not only was I addicted to drugs, but I had also gotten addicted to the streets and all the chaos that came along with it. I had hit a new low!

HITTING ROCK BOTTOM

Most times when people hear the words hitting rock bottom, it's associated with some type of traumatic experience like going to jail or overdosing. It has been "said" that if something so bad happens a person's desired addiction ceases. I had traumatic experiences happen to me several times before and the cravings stayed the same. For me, once the shock of the experience wore off, I went back to my "normal" routine. This leads me to say, everyone who has dealt with addiction experiences is different. For me, hitting rock bottom was my eyes being opened to see the truth of where my choices had taken me.

Little did I know hitting rock bottom would become one of my biggest blessings. I was lower than low. I was lower than an ant crawling on the ground. I was in a place of worthlessness, hopelessness, and helplessness. I was mentally, emotionally, financially, and spiritually broken. I felt like the worst person on the planet. I felt as if my purpose in life was to fail. Could all those negative words planted and spoken over my life by my father be coming to fruition? Nothing in my life reflected anything good, and I didn't see a flicker of hope. What I did see was death in my near future if I did not stop my destructive lifestyle.

The drugs and my wayward lifestyle were catching up to me. I was waking up in unfamiliar places. Not only did I not know where I was, but some nights I did not know how I got there. I started having major chest pains to the point I thought I was having a heart attack, severe headaches, spells of passing out, and bouts of anger and agitation. At the time, I had no clue I was showing all the signs of an overdose. I honestly didn't know if I was going to make it much longer.

One day as I woke up in another strange place, I hurried to find the bathroom. While washing my hands, I looked at myself in the mirror. I did not recognize the person looking back at me. This was my bottom and the point where I started to see the picture of myself everyone else saw. I did not like the lifeless image of the person I saw. At that moment, I was smacked in the face with the reality that doing it my way wasn't getting it. I was as far-off track as a person could get. I had been living in a false sense of reality.

Hitting rock bottom also gave me greater compassion towards others. There is no way I could judge someone else struggling with any hardships in life, whether it be through choices they made or other unfortunate circumstances.

For many years, I believed I could handle my life on my own. Hitting rock bottom let me know I could not handle my life or this addiction on my own. I needed something greater than myself. I needed God!

MOMENTS OF CLARITY

There were times when I did not get high. In those moments, I took time to reflect. I took time to repent. I took time to praise. I SO enjoyed turning on my gospel music and singing praises to God. I listened to "Praise is What I Do" by Shekinah Glory Ministry more than any other song. The song speaks of praising God no matter our circumstances. To praise in the good and the bad. To praise whether happy or sad. There was a part of the song that said, "There is healing and deliverance in the praise. I carried the lyrics in my heart because I believed God for it. These lyrics will forever be embedded in me. I played this song on repeat just to hear the part that said, "my circumstance doesn't even stand a chance, my praise outweighs the bad." I felt in that genuine place of worship, my praise to God overshadowed every bad choice I made. I invite you to listen to the song. I pray it blesses you!

While listening to the song, I would raise my hands and ask God to help me. "Lord, please hear my cry!" I knew my life was on the road to nowhere. I knew what I was doing was wrong. "I don't really understand myself, for I want to do what is right, but I don't do it. Instead, I do what I hate" (Romans 7:15). I knew my actions and behaviors were hurting so many people, including myself. I asked God to forgive me. I begged Him to help me stop living this life of madness. I openly admitted I was an addict, and I knew everything I was doing was a sin. I confessed I was not able to stop on my own. I would also pray for more moments of being able to sing His praises.

When my head was clear, it was evident I NEEDED HELP! This was not the life I wanted for myself. I knew I could not continue to do the same thing and expect a different result. One of two things would eventually happen. One, I would get killed out there on those streets, or two, I would overdose. The common denominator, both scenarios ended in death. I would also reflect on the good times I once had with my family. I wondered if there would ever come a day that we would laugh together again. If they would ever forgive me for all the years of madness and dishonesty. I ended these clarity sessions trusting God. I knew in His way, in His time, He would deliver me.

CHAPTER 4

A GLIMMER OF HOPE

After years of doing drugs and having many near-death experiences, I was over living life my way. Shortly after having another close call with death, I found myself feeling grateful to be alive. I went to one of the spots I would often crash, and I began to sob. In the past, I had other previous close calls with death and "said" I was grateful to live and see another day, but my actions didn't show it. However, something about this experience hit differently. At that moment, I felt like I heard my mother's voice. A small whisper, but I clearly heard "KEEP GOD IN EVERYTHING YOU DO." For the first time in a long time, I felt safe. I felt loved. I felt at peace as I drifted off to sleep. I woke up that morning knowing I had to invite God into the madness with me. This addiction was winning the war for my life. This fight was bigger than anything I had faced. I would not be able to handle this alone.

There was always some form of tragedy present in the pandemonium I lived in. Every day there was a story of someone dying, getting beat up, or going to jail. For whatever reason, people always felt the need to share their hardships with me. This lifestyle was messy. People needed to dump their problems, fears, and concerns somewhere, and I was the person many people felt they could confide in. Personally, I didn't understand why people confided in me. I had my own problems. My life was just as chaotic as theirs. How was I to give advice to others? Did they not realize we were in the same boat? However, I found myself giving advice anyway.

The weight of so many people dumping their problems on me was too much to bear. I had to find a place and/or a person to dump not only my cares and concerns on but the pain of those around me, too. I started to pray. I found myself praying for other people's lives as well as myself.

Two things started happening. First, the more I prayed and gave everyone's situation, including mine, to God, the lighter I felt. In the beginning, I didn't know that giving things to God was called "casting your cares." The Bible says in 1 Peter 5:7, casts all your care upon Him, for He cares for you." Over time I understood the burdens of my life are not mine to bear. I could lay them at God's feet because He cares. Secondly, more opportunities to encourage and listen to others began to present themselves. God blessed me to see a glimpse of who I could become – an encourager. I was a natural-born cheerleader. I was able to find something good in everyone. I began to realize that I also had to encourage myself.

My routine and habits did not change, but my thought process began to. I began thinking and speaking in a positive manner. I prayed and asked God to keep me safe on the streets and to help me make better choices. I began to trust God to deliver me. I chose to believe my life was going to get better. Not only did I believe it, but I also began speaking it aloud. I believed God, being all-powerful would deliver me. I felt the strong urge to speak my deliverance, and my healing, into the atmosphere.

I started speaking words of affirmations over myself. Words of affirmation are any spoken or written words that confirm support, uplift, and empathize with another person in a positive manner. *I am better than this! This is not going to be my end. I am drug-free. I am healthy. I am healed. I am delivered.* I spoke affirmations to myself in the mirror, walking down the street, and when falling asleep. It had been many years since I felt my life could get better. Speaking these positive words over myself continued filling me with greater faith in God. I could no longer keep the words to myself. I then began to share my beliefs with others. I said, "This is not the life God has for me! God has great things for my life." Trust me when I say, talking about God was the last thing people wanted to hear. I ruined many people's high. But at this point, I did not care about how others felt or what they thought. I knew I needed this; literally, my life depended on it. I started to have hope and I did not ever want to lose the feeling ever again. I felt there was true power in saying positive "I am" statements. I chose to change my perspective.

CHAPTER 5

SPEAKING LIFE OVER MYSELF

I called my aunt and asked her if she would pick me up for church. I had not been to church for years. She was so happy to receive my call. She said, "Of course, I will." Let me give you a little back history. After my mom died, I went to church with my aunt. She came and picked me up every Sunday. My aunt's church was nothing like the one I grew up in. The church I grew up in was huge. It had to be over 1200 people in attendance every week. My aunt's church was smaller, and there was more engagement between people. I enjoyed it. Before my madness, I went to church on a regular basis.

Walking through the door of the church after five or six years felt weird. I'm sure everyone at church knew what was going on, considering my aunt would often tell me that everyone said hello and was praying for me. Despite my absence, it felt like I never left. The music was good, the sermon seemed like it was just for me, and the church family genuinely loved on me. I missed being there. I promised everyone, including myself, I would not stay away as long.

I tried my best to fight the temptation of wanting to get high. The first couple of days after attending church when I got the temptation, I would go to sleep. Sleeping used to be one of the coping mechanisms I used when I was in pain or trying to escape reality. However, I could only sleep so much. The third night proved to be much harder. I tried going to sleep to no avail. I fought as much as I could, but the cravings won.

As soon as I submitted to the temptation, I felt guilty. But this time, instead of beating myself up, *I began saying words of affirmations along with a prayer of repentance. This is not the life God has for me, nor is it the life I want for myself. I am a child of God. I am victorious through Christ Jesus. I am who God says I am. I will do what God says I will do. I will be what God says I will be. I am delivered and set free of this addiction.*

I continued to pray every day for God's deliverance. I knew I could not do this on my own strength. One thing that I did know is that if I wanted better, I had to at least try to do better. A wise person once told me, "Do the part you can do, and trust God to do the rest." My part was to say and believe the affirmations, try my best not to get high, and trust God. I did not expect to see or feel any changes happen overnight. It took me years to fall, so I had to understand it would take time for me to stand again. The hope of deliverance was still kindling. Though the flame was small, there was a flame where there once was none.

I continued to attend church a couple of times a month. I began looking for opportunities to get my mind off "self" and focus on encouraging others. I tried to get people in my circle to think about positive times and positive things. I began to pose questions like what do you want out of life? If you could go to a time and place of happiness, what would happiness look like?

Most times our conversations were about how to get money for the next round, but I now wanted to hear about life before they started getting high. I wanted to know their hopes and dreams. Though the same activities were happening, it seemed that some of the heaviness was lifted. We laughed. We remembered when we aspired more.

There started to be moments when everyone was quiet and in thought because of a question I asked. I could see the wheels in their minds turning as they reminisced. Speaking life to them was also speaking life to myself. The affirmations were very powerful for me. They released my negative thinking and kept my mind on what could be. Earlier, I said I did not expect to see or feel any changes happen overnight. However, something was changing. My confidence grew stronger. The confidence that was growing wasn't in myself and my own abilities, but it was in God and His abilities.

Hebrews 11:1 says, "Faith shows the reality of what we hope for; it is the evidence of things we cannot see." My definition of faith is simply trusting God. Trusting God, no matter what it looks or feels like—trusting God in and through all things.

Once while attending church, during the sermon, I heard the pastor say, "God's Word is life." However, I did not understand the meaning. One day, during my moments of clarity, as I was reading my Bible, I came across a scripture that spoke "life" to me. "For I know the plans I have for you," says the Lord. "They are plans for good and not for disaster, to give you a future and a hope" (Jeremiah 29:11). If this scripture was true, the Lord had plans for me even though I was living in madness. Those plans for me were for good and not for disaster, which meant the life of madness I was living would not last always. No matter what the outside circumstances looked like, God would give me a future and a hope. I only needed to believe God would bring this scripture to fruition for me.

Let's fast forward some years. Still here, going through the madness. The thing about it is I knew I was going through it; I did not feel as if I was stuck in one spot. Yes, I was still getting high and making foolish choices, but I had faith the storm would not last always. I lived with expectancy t God would deliver me!

CHAPTER 6

COMING TO THE END OF MYSELF

On February 22, 2010, I woke up and started the day off like every other day. I began planning how I would get everything in alignment for how I was going to get high. I set up the ride, the place to go, and where to purchase everything needed to make this party happen. However, something felt different, but I didn't pause; I kept it moving. I quickly looked in the mirror and said my affirmations. I am healed. I am loved by God. And out the door, I went.

As I walked down the stairs, I remember appreciating the beauty of the day. I took a deep breath and inhaled the cool, crisp air, and while exhaling, I remember feeling peaceful. I got in the car and said, "Today is going to be a good day!" We stopped and got food, ate, and proceeded to pick up our package. All set, ready to get the party started! However, I was hesitant as we all started to sit around the table. However, I eventually sat down.

As I prepared my pipe, it no longer felt right for me. I said, "This is not my life. God has more for me than this!" You could hear the sighs of everyone sitting at the table. One person got up from the table and left the room while someone else said, "Come on, Michele, you've been saying the same thing for years. When are you going to accept this is your reality?" I quickly said, "NO, this is not my life. There's something greater for me!"

I remember getting up from the table, throwing the pipe and the drugs I had in my pocket on the table, and I said, "I'm done!" I walked out the door. Honestly, I do not remember how I got home. Yet, I do remember running to my room, falling on my knees, and surrendering all to Jesus! I said, "God, I need You! I know I've done wrong. Forgive me. Lord, I can't do this anymore! I don't want to go on one more second in this madness. Lord, I can't do it on my own strength. I trust you have the power to deliver me from this! I want You more than these drugs or anything else."

As I laid prostrate, in a pool of tears, I gave God the drugs, the shame and guilt of years of madness, and the prostitution. I gave Him my life. I placed my trust and faith in God alone. At that moment, I could feel God's love surrounding me. I felt the madness leaving my body. The feeling of deliverance surged its way from the top of my head to the bottom of my feet.

When I got up off the floor, there was no doubt I was not the same person that laid down. I was clean. I was free. With one touch from God, I was delivered and set free from 19 years of madness. John 8:36 says, "So, if the Son sets you free, you are free indeed." It is only through the grace of God that I am here today. Because of God's grace for me, I did not have to go to rehab, I did not experience withdrawals, nor did I have the urge to do drugs ever again. I think this quote sums up how I felt: "Grace is when

God gives us good things that we don't deserve. Mercy is when He spares us from the bad things we do deserve. Blessings are when He is generous with both" (Author Unknown).

CHANGE NEEDED

I wasn't deserving of God's grace and mercy, but I was truly grateful. It was important for me to change the people I was around, the places I would go, and the things I would do. I had to be by myself for a while. I wanted and needed to focus on God. I had a lot to process. All the emotions that had been numbed with drugs were now coming alive. They were exposed like a freshly open womb. I had lost the person I once was. Honestly, I asked myself if I ever really knew myself. Did the person before the madness, truly need to resurface? The person I was before was also damaged.

One of the reasons I continued to get high was to conceal all the weight I carried because it was easier to numb the pain than to face it. The pressure to perform as an adult when I was a kid was heavy and too much to bear. I was told how many times I missed the mark and would never come close to hitting it. The negative words spoken over me had scarred my image of who I could be. I believe my addictive tendencies started with food and out of the need to mask the hurt and pain I had during my childhood. There was so much pain, grief, disappointment, and uncertainty that had gone unresolved. Now that I was clean, did I truly know what a "healthy" perspective looked like? I had to learn how to forgive myself for all the pain I had caused myself and so many others. I had to learn how to love myself. I had to gain people's trust back.

All eyes were on me. I felt like a funambulist at the circus as everyone waited in anticipation for me to fall. My family and friends watched every move I made, waiting for the moment I messed up. I wanted to prove to everyone I had changed. I felt I had to live a certain way. I had to do all things well, practice good religion, and become a decent human. I was overwhelmed because I had so much to figure out. I needed to be better than I once was and I once again felt the spotlight was on me to "perform" as others thought I should.

God is so good. He gently placed on my heart that I did not have to continue trying to figure things out on my own strength. 1 Peter 5:7, NLT says, "Give all your worries and cares to God, for He cares about you." Over time, God revealed to me that living for Him was not about religion, but about a relationship. He showed me that I could find rest in Him. God wanted a deep intimate relationship with me. Matthew 11:28–30, MSG says, "Are you tired? Worn out? Burned out on religion? Come to me. Get away with me and you'll recover your life. I'll show you how to take a real rest. Walk with me and work with me—watch how I do it. Learn the unforced rhythms of grace. I won't lay anything heavy or ill-fitting on you. Keep company with me and you'll learn to live freely and lightly. Jesus will remove your heavy burden of guilt and hopelessness and give you true rest in Him."

Just because I knew I was delivered from madness, it meant nothing to those I spent years of my life getting high with. They thought and hoped I was just going through a phase. It seemed once stopped getting high, more invites and more opportunities to get high presented themselves. "No temptation has overtaken you except what is common to mankind. And God is faithful; He will not let you be tempted beyond what you can bear. But when you are tempted, he will also provide a way out so that you can endure it" (1 Corinthians 10:13).

The temptation was all around, but in those moments of temptation, I cried out to God. Sometimes, I thought silently, Lord, help me. While other times, I had to call aloud on the name of Jesus and ask for His help. There was a battle going on inside me, between my fleshly desires and my soul desires. Let me clarify once again. I was set free and delivered. It's not that I wanted to get high; that desire was gone. However, when the opportunities to get high presented themselves, negative thoughts would come. I would hear, "Come on, do it for old time's sake. One hit won't hurt you." It was the voice that guided me and won for years. I had to learn to take those thoughts captive and trust I was not in this battle alone. God was with me.

A couple of months or so after my deliverance, I was walking home from the store and was only a few feet away when a car drove past and quickly backed up. This guy jumped out and said, "Hey Shell, I've been looking for you everywhere. I thought you fell off the planet or moved away. Girl, come on, let's party like we used to." He discreetly pulled out a large quantity of crack. I immediately told him I was no longer getting high. My answer was not acceptable. He was one of the people to who it was hard for me to say no. I said aloud, "Jesus, help me!"

Again, I repeated, 'NO, I do not get high anymore!" Right at that moment, an unfamiliar car pulled up in front of my house. The doors opened, and my daughter and her friends got out of the car. My daughter had come home from college to surprise me for a couple of hours. I had never been so happy to see her. God provided a way out of that uncomfortable, unwanted situation. God is true to His Word. Thank You, Jesus!

The guy quickly said, "See you later, Shel." Praise God, I thought as I embraced my daughter. Shortly after my daughter left, I called everyone on my contact list that I was once associated with during my madness days. I asked them not to call me or stop by anymore. I needed to disassociate myself from everything and everyone that was not walking the same path I was on. I further explained it had nothing to do with thinking I was better than they were. It was for my own mental, physical, emotional, and spiritual well-being. I asked that they respect my decision.

THANKFUL

I am so grateful and blessed by God for who He is and all He has done for me. The more sober-minded I became, the more I realized it was God and only God who carried me during and through the madness. God kept me from the grips of death. I can attest to seven visible times God spared my life. There were many times the devil tried to take me out. "Death wrapped its ropes around me; the terrors of the grave overtook me. I saw only trouble and sorrow" (Psalms 119:3). But God had another plan for my life. God broke the chains that had me bound.

I was delivered from drugs, and God changed my perspective of who and whose I was. I understood the meaning of amazing grace. I was forgiven and redeemed. The song "Amazing Grace" comes to mind. "Amazing grace how sweet the sound that saved a wretch like me. I once was lost, but now I'm found, was blind but now I see." I am so grateful God surrounded me in His love, grace, and protection.

Thank You, Lord, that You never gave up on me. "If a man has a hundred sheep and one of them wanders away, what will he do? Won't he leave the ninety-nine others on the hills and go out to search for the one that is lost (Matthew 18:12, NLT)? Thank You, Lord, that You left the ninety-nine to rescue me. Thank You for loving me as You do. Songwriter Charles Wesley once said, "Had I a thousand tongues, I would praise Christ Jesus with every one of them." I agree with this statement, but I want to add a thousand tongues would not be enough to express my sincere gratitude to my WONDERFUL SAVIOR! Thank You for Your grace, love, and mercy for me. Everything that I am and everything that I shall be is because of You. I am living proof that miracles still happen every day. When God has a calling on your life, no drugs, person, situation, or devil in hell can stop God's plan. I am a witness;

God's Word is true. "No weapon formed against me shall prosper" (Isaiah 54:17).

PRAYER

Prayer changes things. It is a powerful weapon. I am thankful to all the people who prayed for me—the prayers of my mother, my father, my children, and other family members and friends. I am grateful to these people who interceded on my behalf when I couldn't and wouldn't pray for myself. Though my mother is no longer with me, she prayed with the expectation I would do great things for the glory of the Lord. I know her prayers linger on. How great is God that we can come to Him in prayer, no matter the day, hour, or concern?

After being delivered from the madness, I rededicated myself to Christ. I was ready to live for God. For years, I traveled the road of doing it my way. I crashed and burned every time. I had valued myself and my ways over God and His way. No more! I needed and wanted God as the head of my life. I did not want to take one step without Him.

When I surrendered my life to Christ, I surrendered all. I willingly gave God an open invitation to every area of my life. All-access! My life is not my own; it belongs to God. Prayer was becoming an extremely important component of my daily life. I enjoyed having the privilege of being able to go to God with my joys, my fears, and just because He is God. Prayer became one of the best ways for me to share myself with the Lord. The deeper our relationship grew, the more time I wanted to spend with Him.

This is one of the prayers I prayed daily, and it was placed on my heart to share with you. "Lord, thank You for being mighty, loving, and kind to me. I give myself to you today. I surrender my life. I come to You as an empty vessel. Fill me up with the love, patience, strength, mercy, and grace that You have for me. Let me not keep these gifts to myself but pour them out unto others. Align my will to Yours. I come before You Lord with open hands. Everything that You give me to do, say, and be, I give it back to You and ask for Your guidance. Let me love you with all my heart, my mind, and my strength. Let me live a life pleasing to You. A life that brings You glory. Your word says, ask and it will be given, seek and I will find, knock, and the door will be opened. I asked that You fill me up with more of You and less of me. Jesus, thank You again, for being my Savior, my God, friend, and my everything. Thank You for being You. I ask all these things in the name of Jesus. Amen."

MY PURPOSE

After being clean for a couple of years, God reminded me one day about all the positive affirmations that I once said during the years of madness. I thought about the words I spoke over myself. I am who God says I am. I was created with a purpose. I am chosen. The question, "Do you believe the things you spoke?" was placed in my spirit. Some people believe in intuition, but I believe in a higher level of consciousness. Don't get me wrong. I do believe there is a level of intuition that comes from experience. However, as a child of God, I believe the Holy Spirit has a way of communicating with us. This was one of those times. The Holy Spirit helped me understand that God did have a purpose and a plan for my life and that none of my life experiences would be wasted. God revealed to me my purpose was planted long ago. Even before the world was made, God had already chosen me to be His, so that I would be holy and without fault before Him.

I was created to bring God glory, to encourage and to love on His people. "Everyone who is called by my name, whom I created for my glory, whom I formed and made" (Isaiah 43:7, NLT). God planted the calling in me for loving His people at an early age. A couple of months after my mom died, I was feeling down. I decided to take a walk so I could clear my head. As I was walking, I came to a set of railroad tracks where I saw a homeless woman. I felt led to ask her if she needed anything. She said, "Baby, I'm hungry." I told her I would get her food.

I ran home as fast as I could. I made her sandwiches, grabbed bags of chips, sodas, cookies out of the cookie jar, and anything else I thought she would like. I put it in a bag and ran back as fast as I could. I handed her the bag. She quickly grabbed a sandwich and ate it. She looked up at me and thanked me. However, I felt like there was something else that needed to be done. I asked her what else she needed? She said, "What can you do for me?" and, with a chuckle, asked, "How old are you?"

I answered, nine. Again, I said, "Ma'am, what else do you need?"

She said, "I'm homeless. I have nowhere to stay."

I ran home again, grabbed the telephone book, and looked up homeless shelters. I called a couple of places until I found one that offered some assistance. The thing was, she needed to get to the facility to receive help. I called the non-emergency number, explained the situation, and asked if the police would transport her. They said they would. I remember telling the operator that she did nothing wrong; she just needed help and someone to love on her. I ran back and shared with the lady what was going to happen. She chuckled softly and said thank you. I sat with her until the police came. Once the police came, I repeated everything I said to the operator.

I said, "Please, do not take her to jail. She did nothing wrong; she just needs some help." I asked if I could ride along. They told me no and asked how old I was and where my parents were. They collected my information and proceeded to take the lady to her destination. The place she needed to go was about a 10-minute bus ride for me, so I ran home, grabbed money, and hopped on the bus. I wanted to make sure the officers followed through on their word. Thankfully, they did. She needed to be admitted to the hospital and then transported to another facility that had a program to help people get on their feet. I thanked the officers and said my goodbyes to the lady.

I do not remember if I even asked her name. I went home, feeling grateful because I knew that night she would be sleeping in a warm, clean bed. About two to three months later, I received a phone call from the facility that accepted the lady in need. They said they wanted to inform me the lady was there and, on the road, to living a stable life.

I believe God planted a servant's heart in me in my mother's womb. "You made all the delicate, inner parts of my body and knit me together in my mother's womb" (Psalm 139:13, NLT). I have always found great joy in helping others. I do not need anything in return. Helping someone in some way has become an everyday prayer. God graciously blesses me to be able to do it, whether through an encouraging word, lending an ear, or a simple smile while holding the door for someone.

There is nothing like hearing a sigh of relief or seeing the smile on someone's face when an act of kindness is extended. Honestly, I feel a bit selfish because of the joy I feel when I can help someone out. I often wonder who is happier, them or me. I am thankful to God for giving me the privilege and the honor to serve Him and blessing me to bless His people.

PRESENT DAY: HE GAVE ME BEAUTY FOR ASHES

"O all who mourn in Israel, he will give a crown of beauty for ashes, a joyous blessing instead of mourning, festive praise instead of despair. In their righteousness, they will be like great oaks that the Lord has planted for his own glory" (Isaiah 61:3, NLT). For me, ashes represented grief, loss, shame, and despair, BUT GOD. God rescued me from a life of darkness and destruction and gave me life. Through Christ Jesus, I was made whole.

He can also give you peace while going through the storm and heal your broken hearts. Basically, God can take what was old and stale in our lives and give us a renewed and refreshed spirit. I am a living example of God giving beauty for ashes.

God gave me back everything that was stolen from me. God does not waste a thing. Situations we may think are embarrassing, hopeless, or never going to change are all changeable in the hands of Jesus! Where God is, no situation can stay the same. Everything is better with God.

I am thankful to say God brought me from a mighty long way. I am now the Founder and Director of a nonprofit organization called Cornerstone of Grace. Cornerstone of Grace empowers women and children to lift themselves out of life's challenging situations. As a faith-based organization, we serve our families through building healthy relationships, while offering love, discipleship, and resources to build a solid foundation for growth and stability. I want to let women know that they are not that negative voice that tries to define them. Their identity is not found in that "thing" that has them bound. They are not the negative words that may have been spoken over them. They are not the wrong choices they may have made. They are who God says they are.

I am confident in saying You are worthy. You are a masterpiece. You are fearfully and wonderfully made. You can do all things through Christ who is your strength. The reason I know the statements are true is that The Word of God says so.

Let's practice speaking life over yourself now. Say out loud, I am loved by God. I was created by Greatness for greatness. God cares about everything I care about. He who began a good work in me is faithful to complete it

If any of you reading this book are having a hard time believing the words you said aloud, continue saying them. I too once had a hard time believing, but I continued speaking words of life over myself. Eventually, the words took root and became my reality, as they will for you. Proverbs 16:24 says, "Kind words are like honey-sweet to the soul and healthy for the body."

Proverbs 3:5 says, "Trust the Lord with all your heart and lean not on your own understanding but in all your ways acknowledge Him and He will direct your path."

I pray this scripture becomes an anchor scripture for you. You can trust the Lord in all things. Trust Him with all your heart, even when it's hard, trust Him. He will never leave you nor forsake you. Lean not on your own understanding. When life doesn't make sense to you trust Him, when the situation doesn't look good and there seems to be no way out, trust Him. God's word says, "My thoughts are nothing like your thoughts," says the LORD. "And my ways are far beyond anything you could imagine. For just as the heavens are higher than the earth, so my ways are higher than your ways and my thoughts higher than your thoughts" (Isaiah 55:8-9, NLT). In all your ways acknowledge Him. At work, home, school, good and bad times acknowledge Him. Invite Him into every aspect of your life. He will direct your path. That's the promise attached to Proverbs 3:5-6. God cannot go against His word and His promise. So, if God said it, you can trust He will do it.

MY PERSONAL IDENTITY

For many years I saw myself through the lenses of what others said about me. My dad said I was stupid, fat, and worthless. Society said I wasn't good enough or educated enough, mediocre at best. I believed the words spoken over me. I did not feel deserving of anything good. Though my mom spoke words of positivity and life over me, the words of negativity and death my dad spoke over me seemed to smother the words of my mom. Whose root would prove to be everlasting? How thankful I am that I, nor anyone has the final say. God is almighty and is the only one who has the final say! "We can make our own plans, but the Lord gives the right answer" (Proverb 16:1, NLT).

My identity through Christ Jesus trumps every other negative label that was spoken over me. God helped and is still helping me to learn that I am deserving of good things. I am precious in His sight. I am changed. I am loved. I am a child of God. I am rooted in Christ Jesus. The roots of a tree are the foundation. Without the roots, the tree would not be able to grow strong and bear fruit.

The roots of my identity are found in Christ Jesus. To be rooted in Christ means having faith in Him and Him alone. Rooted in Him is also me spending time getting to know who He is and living a faith-filled and dependent life on Jesus. Trusting Him and reading His Word. Inviting Him into my day, my ups and downs. Being rooted in Christ helps me to grow tall and strong like a tree planted along the riverbank, bearing fruit each season. Their leaves never wither, and they prosper in all they do" (Psalms 1:3, NLT). I now understand who I am in Christ Jesus, He is my Solid Foundation and the Ultimate Taproot of my life.

I give God all the glory, honor, and praise because it was not by might, nor by power, but by His Spirit that I am here today, and though I've gone through the fire, I don't smell like smoke! Isaiah 43:2 says, "When you go through the fire, it will not burn you." I want to say never stop believing in God and the power of His love. "But God is so rich in mercy, and He loved us so much, that even though we were dead because of our sins, He gave us life when He raised Christ from the dead" (Ephesians 2:4, NLT).

CONCLUSION

The period of my life where I was dependent on drugs, was not the primary reason I decided to tell my story. Being on drugs was part of the story, but that was not the focus. The purpose of this book is to let you know that God is not a respecter of persons. Which means God does not show favoritism. He loves you just like he loves me. God loves you and is concerned about everything you are concerned about. Nothing you or I could do can separate us from His love. "For I am convinced that neither death nor life, neither angels nor demons, neither the present nor the future, nor any powers, neither height nor depth, nor anything else in all creation, will be able to separate us from the love of God that is in Christ Jesus our Lord." (Romans 8:38-39).

"Plus, I can't keep God's goodness to myself. I MUST tell everyone everywhere the truth of your righteousness. And you know I haven't held back in telling the message to all. I don't keep it a secret or hide the truth. I preach of your faithfulness and kindness, proclaiming your extravagant love to the largest crowd I can find!" (Psalm 40:10-11, TPT). Simply said, I must tell you all the wonderful things God has done for me. Sharing my testimony of God's grace, love, and mercy for me is like fire shut up in my bones. I am passionate about communicating with others all God has done for me

Finally, I want you to know God can use broken people if we only give ourselves and our "madness" to Him. If God can take me, a person once living in darkness and despair, a former drug addict and prostitute, and place my feet on solid ground, He can do the same for you, too. God can take you in your brokenness and use it for His glory. Shelly Hitz, author of Broken Crayons Still Color portrays God using our brokenness so well in her book. She states, "many times what we see as our biggest regrets, failures, and mistakes become what God uses the most in our lives. God transforms our brokenness into something more beautiful than we can even imagine. He takes our mess and creates a masterpiece."

Only God can clean us up, clothe us in His righteousness, help us gain clarity and focus, and put us on the right path. I know I have said this multiple times, but God does have a purpose and a plan for your life. Let me encourage you and say, it does not matter who you are, where you live, or what you have done or are currently doing. God can take the pieces of your broken life and mend them. Only God can reach those places that are torn and tattered. God can take your mess and turn it into a message.

Often, we feel there is no way to be free from the thing that has us bound. Sometimes it seems easier to put a do not enter sign on that part of our lives. However, God can, and He will restore you to newness in Him. Let go and let God into the deepest crevices of your heart. He can heal you physically, mentally, emotionally, and spiritually. There is nothing God can't and is not willing to help you with. No situation is too dirty, shameful, or what we perceive as bad that God's love won't fix.

The wonderful thing is God doesn't love us based on anything we've done or haven't done. He loves us because that's who He is. No matter the labels that may have been placed on you, the level of brokenness, the compulsive behaviors, struggles with identity, or low self-esteem, God will accept you in whatever state you are in. All you must do is surrender your life to Jesus.

To surrender is defined as to give up control of something or to give something up to another. If someone wants to surrender to God, they must willingly relinquish their lives to Him. Therefore, surrender all your brokenness to Him. Just as I invited God into my madness and surrendered, invite God into your (fill in the blank).

My life is worth nothing to me unless I use it for finishing the work assigned to me by the Lord Jesus—the work of telling others the Good News about the wonderful grace of God. If you allow me to give one piece of advice, I will say, if you have not given your life to Christ, please, do so. He is waiting with arms wide open. Trust me you will never be the same.

If you have given your life to Christ, please share your testimony with unbelievers and the gift of life that is waiting for them. And he said to them, "Go into all the world and proclaim the gospel to the whole creation" (Mark 16:15, ESV).

People have asked me if I knew then what I know now about all the trials I would experience in my madness, would I go through it all again. My answer comes quickly. Absolutely! I know some people reading this may think I'm crazy for answering yes. Don't get me wrong, I am not proud of the pain my addiction caused my loved ones. the days of prostitution, or the near-death experiences I encountered. Nevertheless, if I had not reached my lowest point, I would not have lifted my eyes up to Jesus. Today I can praise God because of what was produced through the madness. My intimate relationship with Christ began to bloom, I recognized my need for only depending on Him, my faith in His ability to do the impossible was born, and my desire to do things my way was surrendered. I am no longer ashamed to admit my weakness to God. Where I am weak, He is strong! I praise God for no longer wanting to take matters into my own hands. I am comfortable sliding over to the passenger side to say "Lord, have your way."

I trust God with my life and every victory that comes, I know it is due to God and His ability to do ALL things well. I truly believe all the obstacles, struggles, and challenges I've gone through helped make me who I am today. I am a woman who walks by faith and not by sight.

HOW TO INVITE CHRIST INTO YOUR LIFE

Accepting Jesus as your Lord and Savior does not have to be complicated. When you come to a place of knowing you need God as the head of your life, you can say, "Lord, I need you. I confess I am a sinner and I ask for

Your forgiveness. Jesus, I believe You are the Son of God. I believe You died for my sins, was buried, and on the third day, You rose again. I invite You into my life to be my personal Savior. I want to be fully surrendered to You. I welcome You into my life for the rest of my life."

"If you openly declare that Jesus is Lord and believe in your heart that God raised him from the dead, you will be saved. For it is by believing in your heart that you are made right with God, and it is by openly declaring your faith that you are saved" (Romans 10:9-10, NLT).

"If any man is in Christ, he is a new creature. The old has gone; a new life has begun" (2 Corinthians 5:17, NLT).

AFFIRMATIONS YOU CAN SPEAK OVER YOURSELF

Positive Affirmations are positive statements that can help you to challenge and overcome self-sabotaging and negative thoughts. When you repeat them often and believe in them, you can start to make positive changes.

I Am Enough

I Am Worthy

I Am Growing

I Am Powerful

I Am Beautiful

I Am a Survivor

I Am Safe

I Am Saved

I Am Capable

I Am Happy

I Am Living Expectantly

I Am Forgiven

I Am a Child of God

I Am Strong

I Am Determined

I Am Anointed

I Am Faithful

I Am Kept

I Am Whole

I Am Victorious

I Am Who God Says I Am

I Am Moving Forward

I Am Joyful

I Am Passionate

I Am Unique

I Am Helped

I Am Increasing

I Am Changing for The Better Everyday

I Am Free

I Am Thankful

I Am Delivered

I Am Changed

I Am Patient

I Am Trustworthy

I am Honest

I am Anchored

I Am Rooted

I Am Special

I Am Nothing Without God

I Am Dependent on God

I Am Righteous

I Am Holy

I Am Overflowing with Goodness

I Am Equipped

I Am Bold

I Am Born Again

I Am Open

I Am Available

I Am Hopeful

I Am an Heir

I Am Humble

I Am Privileged

I Am Trusting

I Am Focused

I Am Protected

I Am Excited

I Am Teachable

I Am Gifted

I Am Guided

I Am Powerless Without God

I Am in the Presence of God

I Am Needy (I NEED GOD)

I Am Awed by God

I Am Supported

I Am Valuable

I Am a Masterpiece

I Am More than Conqueror

I Am Who God Says I Am

I Am One of a Kind

I Am Above and Not Beneath

I Am a Lender and Not a Borrower

I Am Talented

I Am a Daughter of A King

I Am a History Maker

I Am a Person with Purpose

I Am a Child of Greatness

I Am a Daughter of Influence

I Am Able

I Am Justified

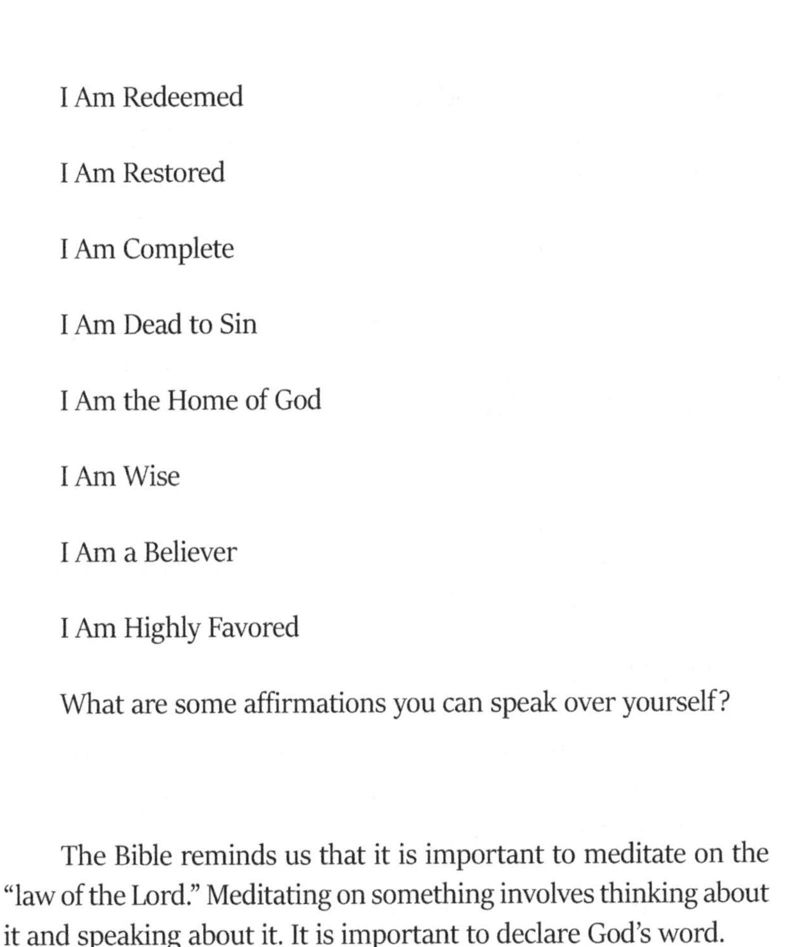

I Am Redeemed

I Am Restored

I Am Complete

I Am Dead to Sin

I Am the Home of God

I Am Wise

I Am a Believer

I Am Highly Favored

What are some affirmations you can speak over yourself?

The Bible reminds us that it is important to meditate on the "law of the Lord." Meditating on something involves thinking about it and speaking about it. It is important to declare God's word.

According to the Oxford Dictionary, a declaration is defined as a formal or explicit statement or announcement.

I Am Loved

- *"And so, we know and rely on the love God has for us. God is love. Whoever lives in love lives in God, and God in them" (1 John 4:16).*

I Am Confident

- *"I am confident of this very thing, that He who began a good work [a]among you will complete it [b]by the day of Christ Jesus" (Philippians 1:6).*

I Am Healed

- *"But I will restore you to health and heal your wounds,' declares the LORD" (Jeremiah 30:17).*

I Am Blessed

- *"Blessed be the God and Father of our Lord Jesus Christ, who has blessed us in Christ with every spiritual blessing in the heavenly places" (Ephesians 1:3).*

I Am Wonderfully Made

- *"I praise you because I am fearfully and wonderfully made; your works are wonderful; I know that full well" (Psalm 139: 14)*

I Am a New Creature

- *"Therefore, if anyone is in Christ, he is a new creation. The old has passed away; behold, the new has come" (2 Corinthians 5:17).*

I Have the Mind of Christ

- *"Have this mind among yourselves, which is yours in Christ Jesus" (Philippians 2:5).*

I Am Not My Own

- *"Do you not know that your bodies are temples of the Holy Spirit, who is in you, whom you have received from God? You are not your own; 20 you were bought at a price. Therefore, honor God with your bodies" (1 Corinthians 6:19-20).*

I Am Hopeful

- *"For I know the plans I have for you," declares the LORD, "plans to prosper you and not to harm you, plans to give you hope and a future" (Jeremiah 29:11).*

"May your roots go down deep into the soil of God's marvelous love" (Ephesians 3:17, TLB).

Cornerstone of Grace - Empowers women and children to lift themselves out of life's challenging situations. As a faith-based organization, we serve our families through building healthy relationships while offering love, discipleship, and resources to build a solid foundation for growth and stability.

Please check out our website at:
https://www.cornerstoneofgrace.org/

Facebook: Cornerstone of Grace

For Interview and/or speaking engagements email me: cornerstoneofgrace3@gmail.com

Made in the USA
Monee, IL
02 February 2024

52836328R00066